Wanderings through the ruins of Heidelberg Castle and its environs. With views. Edited by Richard-Janillon. (From the German by H. J. Grainger.).

Anonymous, H. J. Grainger

Wanderings through the ruins of Heidelberg Castle and its environs. With views ... Edited by Richard-Janillon. (From the German by H. J. Grainger.).

The BiblioLife Network

This project was made possible in part by the BiblioLife Network (BLN), a project aimed at addressing some of the huge challenges facing book preservationists around the world. The BLN includes libraries, library networks, archives, subject matter experts, online communities and library service providers. We believe every book ever published should be available as a high-quality print reproduction; printed on-demand anywhere in the world. This insures the ongoing accessibility of the content and helps generate sustainable revenue for the libraries and organizations that work to preserve these important materials.

The following book is in the "public domain" and represents an authentic reproduction of the text as printed by the original publisher. While we have attempted to accurately maintain the integrity of the original work, there are sometimes problems with the original work or the micro-film from which the books were digitized. This can result in minor errors in reproduction. Possible imperfections include missing and blurred pages, poor pictures, markings and other reproduction issues beyond our control. Because this work is culturally important, we have made it available as part of our commitment to protecting, preserving, and promoting the world's literature.

GUIDE TO FOLD-OUTS MAPS and OVERSIZED IMAGES

The book you are reading was digitized from microfilm captured over the past thirty to forty years. Years after the creation of the original microfilm, the book was converted to digital files and made available in an online database.

In an online database, page images do not need to conform to the size restrictions found in a printed book. When converting these images back into a printed bound book, the page sizes are standardized in ways that maintain the detail of the original. For large images, such as fold-out maps, the original page image is split into two or more pages

Guidelines used to determine how to split the page image follows:

• Some images are split vertically; large images require vertical and horizontal splits.
• For horizontal splits, the content is split left to right.
• For vertical splits, the content is split from top to bottom.
• For both vertical and horizontal splits, the image is processed from top left to bottom right.

Germany   75/2

Wanderings through the Ruins

—

...ght at the Ruins Sunday August 16th 18..

By.

Stanley Dickinson

Belmont Halifax

England

WANDERINGS

THROUGH THE RUINS

OF

HEIDELBERG CASTLE

AND ITS

ENVIRONS.

WITH VIEWS AND PLAN.

———

EDITED

BY

RICHARD-JANILLON,

CASTELLAIN OF HEIDELBERG CASTLE.

———

HEIDELBERG.

PROPERTY OF THE EDITOR.

FROM THE GERMAN

BY

H. J. GRAINGER,

TEACHER OF THE ENGLISH LANGUAGE IN HEIDELBERG.

Carlsruhe. — Chr. Fr. Müller, Printer to the Court. — 1858.

MOST RESPECTFULLY DEDICATED

TO

THEIR ROYAL HIGHNESSES

THE

MOST ILLUSTRIOUS PRINCE

FREDERICK

GRAND-DUKE

AND THE

MOST ILLUSTRIOUS PRINCESS

LOUISA

GRAND-DUCHESS

OF

BADEN

BY THE

Editor.

V

PART I.

WANDERINGS

THROUGH THE

PRINCIPAL BUILDINGS OF THE CASTLE

OF

HEIDELBERG.

I.

PREFACE.

Encouraged by well-disposed patrons and friends, as well as distinguished travellers, to whom either I or my servants, have had the honour of showing the ruins of the castle of Heidelberg, rendered sacred by history and the arts, and to explain to them the interesting historical accounts relating to it, I have taken the liberty of committing to writing my manner of explaining these celebrated ruins, so that every one may be enabled to look into it and judge for themselves.

As Castellain of the castle of Heidelberg, I consider this as a duty I owe to the public; but am far from wishing thereby in my little publication, of enriching the book-trade with a new historical work of the castle of Heidelberg, and what it has experienced; for that I feel I have neither the vocation nor the desire; but (being appointed Castellain of the castle, and having the sole right and duty to show if required, or cause to be shown by persons in my service, all things worthy of being seen in this renowned princely castle), to explain to the tourist who is anxious to know, as exactly and simply as possible, every object of artistical and historical interest in these magnificent ruins, and it being my custom strictly to fulfil the functions of my charge, I have well examined the works written on this subject, and have found, that though they possess merit in many respects, they do not sufficiently answer the object or the demands of the present times so well, as an experience of many years enables me to desire or to exact.

From these reasons, I dare flatter myself, that the numerous visitors to the Heidelberg castle will thank me, if in my wanderings through its ruins, in their present state, I place in their hands a little work, by which they can immediately find their way, — in whatever part of these extensive ruins they may happen to be — and in comparing the letters and figures of that part of the ruins where they may be, with those in my book, they will be enabled to read briefly every thing that is found interesting in it, relative to the spot, where they choose to stop in order to examine it more minutely. Conformably to this I have arranged my walks through the different buildings of the castle in a chronological order, that is, by commencing with the so called OLD BUILDING or RUDOLPH'S BUILDING, known as the most ancient edifice of this castle, which consists of so many buildings constructed at different periods, and will continue them in succession up to the newest constructed works. Consequently I have marked the old building with the letter A, and by means of this letter, will endeavour to describe the same, as well as to mark in the interior of this building, all those interesting spots known in history or tradition, with that letter, and a figure corresponding with the letters and numbers under which I shall describe the different parts of the castle in my wanderings.

The first walk or wandering will contain the principal buildings, each building under its proper letter, in alphabetical order according to the period of its construction; the different compartments of each building with its proper letter, and by figures which will be marked again by *Fig. 1* in each compartment.

To this first walk will follow a second through the fortifications of the castle; and to that a third through the exterior plantations, the gardens and the ornamental works; the whole will terminate with „Wanderings through the environs of Heidelberg", according to the best authorities and my own experience; several friends of the history of our country have likewise had the kindness to advise and help me considerably in the drawing up of this work.

In the wanderings through the fortifications, every remarkable object will be noticed by small letters *a*, alphabetically, while the curiosities of the garden will be enumerated with figures only, and described in the same manner in the book.

I have chosen this chronological arrangement in order to follow up the historical thread in my wanderings, whereby the contemplative pilgrim will often see, reflected as in a mirror, the productions of times past, which is of great interest to the lover of history: and not only to the historian, but likewise to the improving artist, painter, sculptor and architect; and even to the poet and warrior, these ruins are of importance, for one and each of them will find in these objects a particular interest for his profession. However the tourist would take up too much time, if he were to regulate his pilgrimage in the castle, by my chronological wanderings, for he would have sometimes to go from the south, to the north, to the east and to the west; therefore when having finished my wanderings, I shall add to my work, a Guide, in which I shall take care to point out the best way to have a complete view of the whole of the castle, and the reader will only have to refer in his walks, to the explanations of those objects of interest to him, according to the letters and figures in his guide; for the denominations and enumerations of the wanderings and the guide are perfectly arranged alike, and in this manner he will be able to obtain the most detailed accounts of each spot within the boundaries of the castle.

For a further and easier comprehension of these

explanations, I have caused a complete plan of the situation of the castle, its fortifications and plantations to be made out, and added the same to my work, by marking on the place, each building and the other interesting points mentioned in the wanderings by letters and figures, which accompany them in the book, and my respected readers will only have the kindness to compare them with those of the guide.

Many years of experience, of indefatigable and careful research, as well as the frequent request of travellers, and the encouragement of patrons and well experienced friends, have decided me upon undertaking this work.

In my present capacity of Castellain of the castle of Heidelberg, I have caused many interesting parts of these noble ruins, which the destructive hand of time, or the bloody events of long wars have filled up, to be made accessible, and which are of great worth to the history of war, with respect to the fortifications of past times, and have therefore, as far as it lay in my power, not shrunk from making the greatest sacrifices.

Finally allow me to observe, that many travellers have in a most strange manner been led to the illusion, that this superb ruin is the property of a private individual, therefore I consider it my duty for this particular object, to enumerate chronologically at the end of my work a list of those possessors of the castle of Heidelberg, up to the time to when it became a domain of the grand-duchy of Baden.

It appears to me that I have now sufficiently explained the object of my book, and hope to offer to my readers a work worthy of these delightful ruins.

What contemplative man among my readers, can enter this castle, renowned by so many great and unfortunate events, without seeing in it a monument sublime in grandeur, and an object of human weakness, in which the past and the present are united with so many presages? Therefore should this little work, by its brevity and, not by the beauty of its engravings, but by the faithful narration of the destinies of our ruins, be useful, and become acceptable to all visitors, the sole and main object of my wishes will be accomplished.

THE EDITOR.

II.

HISTORICAL INTRODUCTION.

———

Before commencing my wanderings through the magnificent ruins of the castle of Heidelberg, in order to give a more detailed explanation, I consider it a duty I owe to my readers to present to them an historical introduction.

The ancient castle of Heidelberg, an edifice distinguished neither by art nor beauty, nor even of any historical interest, was situated on the little Gaisberg, where at the present time is to be seen a small building in the swiss style, intended for a whey cure establishment, and from whence you have a most delightful prospect — at the present day there are no more traces of this original castle to be perceived; several fragments of its walls were to be seen towards the end of the preceding century, the only remains left of the divers destructions caused by war and the elements. This old castle was built on the ruins of a roman fort, inhabited by Franconian princes in the middle of the XII. century. Conrad of Hohenstaufen, founder of Heidelberg, [1]) as a town, was the first count Palatine of the Rhine who resided there. The very small extent

———

[1]) Not the first count Palatine of the Rhine, as many who have described the castle, have erroneously pretended, for there existed counts Palatine of the Rhine long before Conrad of Hohenstaufen, who did not reside at Heidelberg, but at Stahleck near Bacharach.

of this old castle being [1]) too small for the increasing power of the electors and the counts Palatine of the house of Wittelsbach, or the line of the Schyres [2]) who later obtained the Electoral dignity and possession of the Palatinate of the Rhine; these princes often chose for their residence castles more extensive in the Palatinate, such as Stahleck near Bacharach and others.

But on this same spot, where we still now contemplate, in its ruins the gorgeousness of the new castle, there is said to have existed in the remotest times, a castle founded by the Franconian Prince ANTHYSUS, inhabited later by the Lords of Schlierbach, and there is also mention of an ancient chapel having stood there, where JETTA (according to some historians, the wife of ANTHYSUS), announced her prophecies, and therefore the chapel and the hill on which the latter was built, retained the names of the Chapel-Jetta or Jetta-bühl (Bühl in old German signifying hill). The predictions of Jetta principally related to the future grandeur and glory of the spot. The legend relates that this prophetess of the magnificence of Heidelberg suffered a cruel death, in being torn to pieces by a she-wolf on

---

[1]) In the year 1155 Conrad of Hohenstaufen was invested with the government of the Palatinate of the Rhine by his brother the emperor Frederick I. (Barbarossa); but Conrad's sons died and were buried in the convent of Schönau; so he made over the most part of his estates to female inheritors, because he had a daughter „Agnes" in the bloom of her age, who married HENRY THE GUELPH, son of HENRY THE LION, and who after the death of Conrad, became count Palatine of the Rhine.

[2]) Though Louis I. duke of Bavaria had been invested with the electoral dignity by the emperor Frederick II. of Hohenstaufen, he did not look upon himself as administrator of the Palatinate, and so OTHO THE ILLUSTRIOUS, who married Agnes the youngest daughter of the count Palatine Henry the Guelph, is to be considered the first legitimate count Palatine of the Rhine out of the noble line of WITTELS-BACH, in the year 1225.

the spot where the Wolfsbrunnen or Wolf's-Fountain is now situated.

It is however certain that the experienced searcher of antiquities, will find on examining the ruins more minutely, the remains of walls of a more ancient origin than those of the buildings of the most remote times of the new castle of Heidelberg, and which we will endeavour to make known to our readers in the wanderings.

It appears that towards the end of the XII. century, the count Palatine and elector „Rudolph I." surnamed the Palatine by his contemporaries, formed the plan of constructing a new princely habitation on the Jettabühl, and the quarrels between him and his brother the emperor LOUIS THE BAVARIAN, may have been the cause of its having been fortified. [1])

It may be of peculiar interest to some of our readers to know, that the grandmother of RUDOLPH THE PALATINE, the first founder of our castle of Heidelberg, was AGNES, the eldest daughter of Conrad of Hohenstaufen and his wife Irmengard, a countess of Henneberg. Agnes married HENRY THE GUELPH, son of HENRY THE LION, duke of Brunswick, and bore him a son HENRY THE YOUNGER — who married Mathilda of Brabant, and died without heirs — and two daughters, the eldest of whom Irmengard, married the margrave HERMANN OF BADEN; and AGNES the younger, married OTHO THE ILLUSTRIOUS, son of LOUIS THE BAVARIAN of the house of Wittelsbach in 1225, out of which latter marriage, the possession of the beautiful Palatinate of

---

[5]) Abbot VOLKMAR OF FÜRSTENAU, a contemporary of RUDOLPH I., and one of the oldest historians of Bavaria, relates that Rudolph having heard of the victory his brother LOUIS had gained over Duke FREDERICK OF AUSTRIA, left Munich with all his family and court to come and live at Heidelberg.

the Rhine was secured to the princely house of the Schyres, (the only brother Henry the Younger having died without issue) whereas Irmengard, by right of birth, ought to have succeeded to it. This female ancestor of the illustrious family of the princes of Baden, IRMENGARD the noble daughter of the GUELPH, founded „Lichtenthal" a convent of the Cistertians, near Baden-Baden in the year 1245, of which, after the death of her husband margrave HERMANN OF BADEN, she became the first Abbess, and was interred in the vaults there after her decease.

The princely houses of Bavaria and Baden consider these two sisters Irmengard and Agnes as their maternal ancestors, and what the children of the Baden ancestry were deprived of, the inscrutable decrees of providence restored nearly six centuries afterwards to the later descendants of Irmengard.

It was a fortunate idea of RUDOLPH I to found a princely residence on a moderate height of 300 feet [1] above the surface of the Neckar, where the eye enjoys one of the most delightful views that can be imagined, and which in the course of centuries, had been raised by its splendour and magnificence, above all the other residences of the countries of Germany, and still excites, by its ruins, the admiration of all visitors. [2]

Go, pilgrim and wander on a fine summer's day, through the shadowy alleys of the castle gardens, and thine ear will be struck with sounds of almost all the european languages; but what is it, that attracts such numerous strangers from all parts of the compass?

---

[1] The castle of Heidelberg is situated 613 feet above the level of the sea.

[2] The space which the grounds of the ruins of the castle, its fortifications and gardens occupy, consists of about 40 acres of land, which is out of proportion to the considerable bounds the precincts of the castle formerly possessed.

Is it the great erudition of the ancient university of Rupert? Is it the hospitality of the inhabitants of Heidelberg? or is it the bacchanalian delights of the great tun of Heidelberg, that have such mighty attraction? Alas! the latter is empty, and the others may perhaps contribute to it in some measure; but it appears to me above all, that the only magnetical force of attraction of Heidelberg consists in its paradisiacal situation, blessed with a healthy climate, and adorned, with the most majestic ruins of Germany, or, I may say, of the whole world.

I conclude my introduction with the words of the poet Kotzebue:

„If an unhappy individual were to ask me what spot he would live in, to get rid of the cares and sorrows which pursue him, I should say Heidelberg; and a happy one ask me what spot he would choose to adorn with fresh wreaths the joys of his life, I should still say Heidelberg.“

III.

WANDERINGS

THROUGH THE PRINCIPAL BUILDINGS OF THE CASTLE OF
HEIDELBERG.

———

A.

THE OLD- (or RUDOLPH'S) BUILDING.

This venerable building, which (to judge from the
history of the Palatinate) had already been projected by
the male ancestor of all the successive Dukes, Pals-
graves and Electors, Rudolph I., the Palatine, of the
ancient house of Wittelsbach, must have been inhabited
during the first part of the XIV. century, for several
documents of this prince have been found, dated 1308;
but the castle on the Jettabühl is only expressly mentioned later, in the treaty of Pavia 1329, where it is
said: „the upper and lower castle, and town of Heidelberg". Consequently this venerable building was the
necessary commencement of the later majestic castle,
and even to-day, the lineal descendants of its first builder occupy the regal thrones of Bavaria and Greece.

The primitive building extended from the south to
the north, and its principal front to the west, from
where the Jettabühl descends steeply; for the high rampart on this side, which now raises its gigantic walls
above the deep moat, was only constructed at a later
time, which I shall report in its proper place.

Elector RUDOLPH I. was son-in-law to the unfortunate Emperor ADOLPH of Nassau, to whom he was attached by extraordinary affection and loyalty, consequently he was involved in many fights; soon after the decease of his father-in-law, and the succeeding Emperor HENRY VII., the Luxemburgher, he by proxy gave his elective vote for the Emperor, to Duke FREDERICK OF AUSTRIA, and not to his brother LOUIS the BAVARIAN.

Even at that time, the new castle must have been strongly fortified, on account of the frequent feuds of its builder.

RUDOLPH I. felt all the effects of the anger of his brother, now elevated to the imperial dignity; he was obliged to fly from his country, to wander about sick and destitute of support, and died an outlaw in a foreign land.

In such manner did this first building suffer under its founder; and if these cold stones could speak, what horrible tales could they not unfold to us of what has passed beneath them!

The springers and mouldings which are still to be seen before the Rudolph's-building, formerly composed the base of a fountain furnished by pipes, in the middle of which was a column, with a lion rampant on the top, bearing in its fore feet the arms of the Palatinate; this fountain was undoubtedly the most ancient of the castle. (A. 1.) It is only from the foundation that the modest commencement of the castle of Heidelberg is to be perceived. These caves consist chiefly of places appropriated to the cellars and different offices of the castle.

The fanciful visions of certain romance writers, that these subterranean vaults were used as the seat of secret criminal justice (Vehmgericht), so much feared in those times, are nothing but imaginary dreams, devoid of all historical foundation.

14

The first story contained many apartments; and
there are still to be seen the remains of an old fresco
painting of the entry into the castle of Pope John XXIII.
(Balthazar Cossa) as prisoner, who was for a time
confined in this dreary spot. From the windows of this
papal prison (*A. 2*) is to be seen the place where the
Tennis-court was afterwards erected; at the time of
Louis III. who held Pope John XXIII. as prisoner, the
old wall of the fortress could be seen, and beyond that
the wide open country. Now this Tennis-court is converted into a delightful garden.

The unfortunate ex-pope sang of his sad captivity
in a beautiful poem which is still extant, beginning
with these words:

„*Qui modo summus eram, gaudens et nomine praesul,
Tristis et abjectus nunc mea fata gemo.*"

(*A. 3.*) The second story contained, together with some
insignificant apartments, the celebrated regal chamber,
in which at the commencement of the XV. and XVI.
centuries, the court-festivities and other ceremonies were
celebrated.

(*A. 4.*) At the end of the passage in the second
story, we perceive the remains of a beautiful winding-
staircase, which formerly conducted from the apartments
of the upper stories, to the Rupertina Chapel, built
nearly half a century afterwards; by a new wooden
staircase, you ascend to the third story, and in this,
in a large archway to the west, opposite to one towards
the east, is a beautiful balcony in the gothic style, with
a view over the large castle yard, and which belonged
to the oldest part of the buildings of this wing of the
castle (*A. 5*).

From this balcony, it is said, that LOUIS THE BEARDED,
father of FREDERICK THE VICTORIOUS, often witnessed
the joyful sports of his princely sons. Old people remember having seen at the beginning of this century,

the windows of this balcony still ornamented with painted glass. Near this balcony is a little apartment with a niche (*A. 6*) in which, most probably, there was formerly a house-altar. It is here that Lo'uis III. the Bearded, on his return from Palestine, is said to have had his oratory. The other apartments were appropriated to the family of the Counts-Palatine.

The staircase marked *A. 4* also led to the third story, for the door way to the west is still to be seen, and which conducted to the upper stories; but let us return to the heirs of the unfortunate founder.

After the death of the hostile brother, the enmity of the emperor Louis ceased, and he took a paternal interest in the sons of Rudolph I.; and reinstated them into a greater part of their inheritance; whereupon Adolph (1327) with his brothers Rudolph II., and Rupert I. and their mother Mathilda entered into possession of this castle.

Soon after, the elector Adolph died (1329), but during his life time ceded the government to his brother Rudolph II., who reigned peacefully for 26 years, and died revered and happy in (1353), when his brother Rupert I. succeeded him in the government, of whose actions and operations we shall have much to relate in the following section, and we have only now to add, that the old building of Rudolph was destroyed in the war of succession, in (1689), by count Melac, the destructive angel of the Palatinate.

B.

THE RUPERTINA-CHAPEL or THE COOPERAGE.

Even before Rupert I. had commenced to reign, he founded the University of Heidelberg in 1346—1386; in the course of the first year (1346) he also founded the old court-chapel, and dedicated it to St. Ulderich, at that time Bishop of Augsburg, and later it became celebrated for its magnificence and riches. In the XVI. century its revenues amounted yearly to 350 ducats, a most considerable sum at that period. The Elector Philip likewise caused mass to be said here every Martinmas for the souls of those warriors who fell in the battle of Seckenheim, under his uncle FREDERICK the Victorious.

The communicating staircase (*B. 1*) mentioned under *A. 4*, which is almost entirely preserved, and led from the apartments of the princes from the Rudolph's-Building to this sacred edifice, was built by RUPERT I. When you are alone amongst the deserted walls of the so-called cooperage, you may still see to the right the remains of gothic windows, which once ornamented a lateral chapel (*B. 2.*)

On the elevation which leads from the great hall to the afore mentioned gothic windows, the Count-Palatine FREDERICK II., was married on the 9th of March 1535 to the danish princess Dorothea, by Philip Bishop of Spire; and on the 23rd November 1551, the Count of Hanau to the Princess-Palatine Helena.

Under Rupert I., this meritorious prince, who died at a very advanced age in 1390, our castle underwent many enlargements and improvements.

If nothing now remains of the former splendour of the Rupertina Court-Chapel, but cold walls, which mark the place formerly consecrated to devotion, Rupert I. erected a monument in another building, which flourishes still unto this day in all its prime, and which has imparted so much knowledge to the world, I mean the UNIVERSITY OF HEIDELBERG, and in whose crown, the pearl of science and the stone of wisdom form the most precious jewels.

When in 1348 the south of Germany was ravaged by a dreadful epidemic disease, which the people in the

RUPERTUS
SENIOR
MCCCXC

blind superstition of that period, attributed to the Jews, accusing them of having poisoned the wells, whereupon they where persecuted, put to the torture, and assassinated in the most cruel manner; the chroniclers of those days state, that at that time, 12,000 of those unfortunate wretches were massacred in Germany; then it was that the noble and generous Elector Rupert I. took pity upon these unfortunate people, offered them an asylum in his country, and protected them from all further persecutions.

When you, respected wanderer, stand in the courtyard, and cast your eyes up towards the south corner of the cooperage, you will see the most ancient coat-of-arms of the Palatinate in all this great castle.

This building underwent a complete transformation in 1615.

FREDERICK V. changed it into a regal hall, to celebrate the court festivities and his nuptial ceremonies, adorned his new creation with mythological figures, instead of the former sacred pictures, and transformed the upper building into dwellings.

(*B. 3.*) Four colossal pillars, the basements of which, the wanderer may still perceive in these vast ruins, bore the vaulted roofs of this, the greatest hall in the whole castle; but this sumptuous palace was not of long duration; the Swedes endeavoured to destroy it in 1634, and though it was restored afterwards by CHARLES LOUIS in 1658, and furnished with high gable walls, it was entirely destroyed by the French in 1689 and 1693, and only in order to secure the cellars which are underneath this building, CHARLES PHILIP in 1716 caused a scanty roof to be constructed, and a staircase (*B. 4*) to be built, which disfigured the whole communicating with the new church, the upper parts of which are still to be seen in ruins.

CHARLES THEODORE at last had the remains of the

walls covered with the roof which still exists, and converted the same into a cooperage.

The high windows were afterwards nearly all walled in, like most all the openings of the castle, whereby the interior space not only became dark, but likewise damp and unhealthy; consequently I had the windows re-opened, and the winding staircase, mentioned above under *B. 1*, cleared away from the rubbish, and thereby caused a free circulation of air.

You may still see, respected wanderer, at the north-west extremity of the hall, the remains of the foundation of a tower (*B. 5*), which formerly ornamented the Rupertina-Chapel, whereas to the north-east, you may see the remains of a beautiful winding staircase (*B. 6*), which formerly led from the chapel to the upper and lower stories.

Having finished relating the fate of this building, let us now return to the course of our chronological account.

After the death of RUPERT I., he was succeeded by Rupert II., surnamed the Hardy, the son of his brother ADOLPH THE SIMPLE, under whose government the castle was not enlarged; but after the decease of this prince in 1398, he was succeeded by his only son RUPERT III., the builder of the church of the Holy Ghost at Heidelberg, a magnanimous prince, who gained the esteem and affection of the whole of Germany, and who was inspired with a love for arts and sciences.

He did more for the enlargement and improvement of this castle, than the five regents who preceded him, by enriching it with one of the most celebrated architectural monuments of the castle, that is to say, he added to the south-side of the „Old Building", a new and more magnificent one, which he extended farther to the court towards the east, in a parallel direction to the Rupertina-Chapel, and which is called to this day:

C.

THE RUPERT'S BUILDING.

We must first make known to our wanderer through the ruins of this castle, a few incidents out of the glorious life of the founder of this building.

RUPERT III. was born on the 5th May 1352 and succeeded to the government in his 46th year; he was not only much revered by his people, but by almost all his fellow princes, received from his contemporaries the surname of „THE GOOD“, and on account of his strict love of justice, that of a „JUSTINIAN“.

When King WENCELAUS, the Idler, son of the Emperor CHARLES IV. was dethroned, the assembly of the Electors at Boppart, lower Rhine in 1400, unanimously declared the Elector Rupert III. to be KING OF GERMANY.

But the modest castle of Rudolph I., was now too small for the court of a German King; for he was often obliged to hold his court in the convent of the Augustines at Heidelberg, because his paternal residence was not sufficiently large. It was then that the King undertook the building of his new castle, which he erected at the side of the Rudolph's building, to the south, and it is supposed that already in 1406, he went to live there with his family, for it was in that year he protected the university against the attacks of the higher nobility and citizens of Heidelberg, and gave here, from his new castle, sound and efficacious laws for the future security of this learned foundation. As we have said before, the church of the Holy Ghost, owes its origin to this prince.

King RUPERT was married to ELISABETH, daughter of the Burgrave FREDERICK OF NUREMBERG, who bore him four sons, the future founders of the four lines of the Palatinate, one of which is preserved to the present day, and still reigns upon the thrones of BAVARIA and

GREECE. Returning from a journey home to his residence in Heidelberg, this great German King met with his death, at the castle of LANDESKRON, near OPPENHEIM, after which his mortal remains were deposited in the vaults of the church of the Holy Ghost at Heidelberg, from which last resting place they were dragged out by the murderous troops of his MOST CHRISTIAN MAJESTY, Louis XIV. (1689) and this tomb worthy of veneration, was demolished.

I will now lead the wanderer into the interior of this building, but must first show him some works of sculpture, which adorn the front.

Over the gothic entrance, respected wanderer, if you cast up your eyes, you will observe a symbolic figure, under the form of a wreath of roses, in the middle of which is to be seen a pair of compasses half open representing an A, the whole supported by two angels.

Without any prejudice to other explanations, this most beautifully worked figure seems to me to be a mystical sign of those old corporations or guilds of architects, who by their united strength and talents, have produced such magnificent works of architecture of the middle age. The half-opened compasses, under the form of an A appears to note the beginning of all things, as well as their destination, to produce a circle, is the symbol of eternity, which has neither beginning nor end, but in which all things, even this building was created.

The sacred number of the five roses drawn up into a round garland, denotes the flourishing of the building; while the angels appear to announce that only a higher wisdom alone can transform terrestrial roses into celestial flowers worthy of eternity, for all the works of this world generally become, sooner or later, a certain prey and sacrifice to time. The master of the works of the RUPERT'S-BUILDING, must have also been employed in the building yard of the cathedral of Strasburg, for in a lateral building of the Minster (seminarium) as well as in the church of the Holy Ghost, the same mystical sign is to be observed. Others say again, that this sign is nothing but an emblematical representation of the well known motto of Rupert *(fiat justitia etc.)* by the wreath of flowers denoting the world, the compasses justice, and the angels the world to come.

The loud rejoicings and the merry-makings which formerly used to fill these vast halls, have now ceased, the sumptuousness of these apartments disappeared, and their owners crumbled into dust, within their sepulchres.

How beautifully Mathisson expresses himself on this subject:

> Hoheit, Ehre, Macht und Ruhm sind eitel!
> Eines Fürstenhauptes stolzer Scheitel
> Und ein zitternd Haupt am Pilgerstab
> Deckt mit einer Dunkelheit das Grab.

> Rank, honour, might and fame are vain!
> The proud crown of the prince's head,
> And a trembling head, leaning on a pilgrim's staff,
> Both are covered with like obscurity in the grave.

Further you may perceive to the left of the entrance of the old grey walls of this venerable royal domain, the arms of King RUPERT in a stone bas-relief. A plain eagle of the house of Germany spreads its wings, under which are seen two smaller escutcheons, the LION of the PALATINATE, which the ancient Counts-Palatine had adopted from the former Dukes of FRANCONIA; and the chequers of Bavaria; a little further to the left you will find a tablet of stone, of later origin, placed there by the Elector Frederick II. with the following inscription in old German:

> Tausend vierhüdert Jar mā zelt
> Als pfalzgraf Ruprecht wart erwelt
> Zu Römischem kong uñ hat regirt
> Uff zehen Jar darin volnfirt

Dis hauss welches pfalzgraf Ludwig
Erneuert hat wiess stedt lustig
Der jm vier und viertzigsten jar
Fünffzehe hundert auch fürwar
Uss disser welt verschieden ist.
Ir baider seln pfleg Jhesus Christ.
Amen.

Underneath it is dated 1545.

Now, wanderer, follow me through the gothic gate into the interior of the building, where we shall enter a vestibule (*C. 1*) and to the left a hall in the beautifully formed cross vaults of which the key-stones are ornamented with shields on which the plain imperial eagle of the King is quartered with the crowned lion of the Palatinate, the chequers of the Duchy of Bavaria, the shield of Wittelsbach argent and azure crossed, and that of Zollern. This is now called the Knights-Hall or Armoury, and filled with armour, helmets and swords, but which have no relation at all to the history of the castle. The other objects were all found in the ruins or within the precincts of the castle.

This hall may formerly have served as an assembly room (*C. 2*) of the princes and the court, while the space to the right, as you enter the building, where several fragments of stones are preserved, as an assembly room for the nobles and vassals.

In the back ground of the vestibule, the beautiful winding staircase of the castle will lead you to an octagon tower in the upper stories, where you will immediately enter to the right, into the large dining room and PRINCES' HALL of that period (*C. 3*); which a few years ago was buried in ruins and dirt, and now newly transformed into a modern, but much smaller hall. The walls of this apartment are decorated with paintings and antiquities, relating to different circumstances which have taken place in this curious castle, and in some measure are of historical worth; even in the time of king Rupert, this hall was ornamented with the portraits of his ancestors and relatives, in the middle of which was the portrait of his forefather OTHO.

The most interesting of all these ruins of past grandeur, are the remains of a colossal hearth *(C. 4)* which formerly spread its heat over the large dining-room. These ruins are all that are left of that magnificence which is said to have existed all over this royal apartment. What we can still see of the chimney piece, is covered over with figures in bas-relief, unfortunately mutilated by that destructive hand of time that respects nothing. Above the chimney-piece you will see two lions, one carrying the arms of the electors Palatine, and the other those of the kingdom of Denmark, for the wife of Frederick II. (of whom we shall have an opportunity of giving a more detailed account), was Dorothea, daughter of Christian II. of Denmark. You will further see in the arms of the Palatinate, the order of the golden Fleece and the imperial orb, the former of which Frederick II. received of the emperor Charles V. The principal shield quartered with the royal arms of Dorothea, will show you the emblems of three kingdoms of the north, at that time united under one sceptre. In the middle shield, likewise quartered, you will see the armorial bearings of those lands which came in succession to the royal house of Denmark, such as: the crowned lion azure of Schleswig; and the nestle argent, with the three nails argent, in a red field, of Holstein; the swan argent, of the county of Stormarn, and the cross-beams of Oldenburg.

The two busts near to the arms of Dorothea, represent her royal parents, Christian II. and his wife Isabella, sister to the emperor Charles V.; the two others, on both sides of Frederick's arms, represent the emperor CHARLES V. crowned with laurel, and his wife ISABELLA, daughter of king EMANUEL OF PORTUGAL.

Several shields in this interesting work are, as afore
mentioned, much damaged; of the inscription on the
chimney-piece we can only read:

„ . . . . . CHURFÜRST DER HAT
. . . WERCKH WIE ES HIE STAT
. . . . . AUFRICHTEN LON
SEIN REGIMENT WOLL LANG BESTON.“

„ . . . . . Elector who has
. . . . . Work like this is
. . . , . . . to be constructed
May his reign last long.“

The inscription under Dorothea's arms is still entirely legible, and runs thus:

SEIN GEMAHEL VON KONGLICHEM STAMM
FRAW DOROTHEA IST IHR NAM
GEBORN PRINZESSIN AUS DENEMARKH
NORWEGEN, SCHWEDEN, DREI KÖNIGREICH STARCKH.

His wife of royal ancestry
Dame Dorothea is her name
Born princess of Denmark
Norway, Sweden, three mighty kingdoms.

In the centre entablature you will perceive a death's
head, on the sides of which are two poppy-stalks with
two serpents, between them an hour-glass on a child's
head; all these are allusions to life, the sleep of death,
the resurrection, and the transfiguration. This work was
finished in 1546. But before we proceed to enumerate
the curiosities of this room, we must recontinue the
thread of our history.

After the decease of king RUPERT, his son LOUIS III.,
or as his contemporaries called him, on account of his
great beard, „the Bearded“, succeeded him in the
government, while his three brothers, JOHN, came
into possession of the Upper-Palatinate, STEPHEN of
Mosbach, and OTHO of Simmern and Deux-Ponts.
LOUIS III. was the father of FREDERICK the Victorious,

already mentioned in the description of the Rudolph's building. This elector was obliged to appear at the celebrated council of Constance, as the representative of the emperor Sigismund and as judge of the empire, which placed him in many a disagreeable situation; he was obliged for instance, as judge of the empire to conduct the trial of the unfortunate professor at Prague JOHN HUSS, and to bring him as prisoner with him to Heidelberg, and Pope JOHN XXIII., BALTHAZAR COSSA, whom he kept confined as captive in Rudolph's building (already mentioned in the description), till he had him transported later to EICHOLZHEIM near MANNHEIM.

This elector likewise enlarged the residence on the Jettabühl, by purchasing an adjoining garden and a ditch. Blindness and the gout closed the latter days of LOUIS, and even during his lifetime he confided the reins of government to his brother OTHO, as guardian to the electoral prince LOUIS (1436), but however LOUIS THE BEARDED died soon after (1437).

At the commencement of the year 1442 LOUIS IV. assumed the government in the eighteenth year of his age; he was a prince of an exceeding mild and benign character, married when very young MARGARET OF SAVOY, who bore him a son, the succeeding elector PHILIP, and died after a short reign in 1449; upon which FREDERICK the Victorious, brother of LOUIS IV., acted as guardian to his nephew, who was scarcely one year old; but already in 1452, the nobles of his land [1]) decided upon his accepting the electoral dignity, whereupon he adopted his nephew, making a vow never to

---

[1]) Among these nobles, v. Gemmingen, v. Sturmfeder, v. Böcklin, v. Vitzthums, v. Wambold, v. Handschuhsheim, v. Venningen, v. Berlichingen, v. Helmstatt, v. Walbron and others particularly distinguished themselves.

marry, at least, with right of equality of birth to his issue. History seldom relates to us of a prince so celebrated for his brilliant exploits.

It is in this regal hall, where FREDERICK, afterwards called the Victorious, feasted the princes, counts and nobles, whom he had made prisoners after the battle of Seckenheim; but though the tables were loaded with viands of every description, bread, the most necessary article for a meal, was wanting; and when the captive nobles timidly requested the same, the victorious Frederick rose with a serious air, pointed out to them from the windows of the hall, the still reeking ruins of the villages, the trodden fields of those former beautiful and fertile plains, which used to present to the contemplative eye of the beholder from these windows, a smiling garden, radiant with brilliant freshness, and said, „The warrior who wantonly lays waste the harvest and the mills of the peaceful countrymen, deserves no bread! Take now as a warning example, that silly rage is unworthy of a noble, that punishment generally falls back upon those, who have engendered it by their cruel inhumanity and insatiable pride. To you it shall be measured with the same bushel, as ye have measured it to others.“

But not only did the victorious laurel surround the brow of Frederick, but it was likewise through the olive branch of peace that he sought to raise art and science, and the myrtle of love did not refuse him its wreath.

A beautiful poetess of Augsbourg, the noble CLARA OF DETTIN, fully returned his love, and became his spouse, from which union issued the princely house of LÖWENSTEIN-WERTHEIM, and which still exists to the present day.

Many of the outerworks, particularly the blown-up tower to the south-east, which we shall more explicitly detail further on, as well as other fortifications, owe their existence to this glorious prince.

But already in the year 1476 he died, he, whom his enemies called „the wicked Fritz", but to whom his contemporaries gave the name of the MARCUS AURELIUS of his century. He had scarcely exceeded the age of manhood when he died; and was buried, according to his wish in a simple garment, in the convent of the Barefooted-Friars in Heidelberg; and even there his remains could find no peace, which during his life for so long a time in vain had sought for rest; for two centuries after, the murderous troops of the French at that time, during the wars of the Palatinate, dragged his bones from out of their silent tomb, and scattered them for the most part to the dust.

His nephew the elector PHILIP THE SINCERE, succeeded him, who already in his youth had courageously seconded the enterprises of his heroic uncle. The future days of his government were not so fortunate as those of his great uncle; the God of war was not so propitious, and the war of succession of the house Palatine of Bavaria, on account of the territories of his son's father-in-law, LOUIS THE RICH OF LANDSHUT-BAVARIA, against his cousin the duke of Bavaria, did not terminate in favour of the elector, and soon after the fatal war of 1508 he fell a victim to his sufferings, not quite sixty years old, at Germersheim, from whence his body was brought to Heidelberg and interred there in the church of the holy-ghost.

This noble elector was devoted to the muses; several of his poems are still preserved, one of which we will only mention here.

He once wrote to a monk whom he much esteemed, and who had begged him for a few verses from his own hand, the following in elegant latin:

„Des Klosters Einfalt kann vortrefflich mir behagen,
  Wenn unter dunklen Kutten reine Herzen schlagen;
  Doch unter dunklem Kleid auch Falsches zu ersinnen,
  Weh', welch' ein Ungethüm! schwarz aussen und von innen!"

„The convent's simple manners may become my part,
  If the dark frock conceals a purely beating heart;
  But should a wicked organ this dark cloak conceal,
  A monster, black without and black within I'd feel."

At the time of this prince, the knights of the Rhine held a grand tournament to his honour, which was the thirtieth in the order of succession of these celebrated exercises of arms. The worshipful the knights of the Ass dedicated it to the four countries of German knighthood. It was then, that the halls and saloons of the Rudolph- and the Rupert-Buildings swarmed with princes, counts and knights, with fair wives and chaste damsels; the most beautiful and virtuous ladies distributed the prizes of the lists to the bravest knights, after which the joys of the banquet commenced amidst the lights of a thousand lamps and torches and to the sound of trumpets. Who now dreams in contemplating these sad ruins, surrounded with mourning ivy, of the joys and splendours of those days gone by.

Louis V. succeeded his noble father, and endeavoured as a wise man to heal those wounds which the unhappy war of the Bavarian palatine succession had brought upon his lands, and from a passionate love for architecture, undertook to enlarge his castle considerably.

Before we conclude our notes on the Building, which owes its existence to the German King and Roman Emperor RUPERT [1]), we must relate an anecdote in his life, which history has preserved up to our times, and which gives us an opportunity of judging of the good natured character of this great prince.

----

[1]) Rupert, as already mentioned, was chosen king at Boppart in 1400.

When he returned from Rome in 1403 after his coronation as Roman Emperor, the children of Heidelberg
received him in their festive garments, singing hymns
which they had learned by heart unto his praise: it hap-
pened that here and there they faltered, or occasionally
sung out of tune, for which their zealous teachers punish-
ed them with cuffs and blows, which the kind emperor
by chance perceiving, caressed the little ones, and turning to their teachers, said to them in gentle reproach:

„Do not threaten nor beat these dear children; for
the Lord said: Suffer little children to come unto me,
for theirs is the kingdom of God! Rather let us praise
the Lord our God, that out of so many dangers he has
brought us back again to our dear children.“

A glance into the cruel manner of carrying on the
war at that time, may in some way vouch for the manner of acting of this otherwise noble prince, when at
Spire in 1388 after a brilliant victory over his enemies,
he caused 60 incendiaries among his prisoners to be
thrown into a lime-kiln, saying:

„Under the favor of the night, you have put my
poor people to the sword and flame, I will now send
you in broad daylight to the smoke.“

D.

THE BLOWN-UP TOWER.

So is a certain tower generally called, which I shall
mention more explicitly in my wanderings through the
fortifications, and only notice here in speaking of the
principal buildings, that it was constructed by FREDE-
RICK I., the Victorious, in the middle of the XVth cen-

tury, and now forms one of the most picturesque parts of the castle ruins.

This prince, who for the most part of his reign was almost always in the heat of action, was forced to think of rendering the castle of his fore-fathers as strong as possible for that epoch, so he built this tower with walls of a colossal thickness, as well as two other towers, the primitive foundations of which now only are remaining; these three towers served to fortify the eastern part of the castle. Originally only the lowest parts of the tower were vaulted over, the others consisted of wooden flooring, resting on mouldings, and the whole covered with a high wooden pointed roof; FREDERICK IV. first caused the upper parts to be vaulted over, and pillars to be placed in the centre, for the greater safety of the edifice; he likewise built the octagonal superstructure with its open gallery, and gave it a roof in the shape of a dome.

This tower will ever remain as a monument of the rage for destruction, with which France at that time carried on the war against the unfortunate Palatinate; from the time of its explosion, which now gives it such a picturesque appearance, it has generally been called the „blown-up tower“, for a further description of which I beg my respected readers to refer to my „wanderings through the fortifications“.

E.

THE LOUIS-BUILDING.

Opposite to the Rupert's-Building, the Elector Louis V. erected a new palace, and to this he further added the kitchen- and household-departments, worthy of such a princely castle. The Elector Philip had already drawn up the plan for these buildings, and according to old documents is said to have laid the foundation stone. The Louis-Building formerly extended to the middle of the palace of OTHO HENRY, and in its ruins the noble traces of its former splendour are still to be seen; but now the dwelling apartments of the Elector LOUIS V. occupy but very little space, and only comprise the old grey wing, which extends in three stories to the octagon tower, upon which over a gothic doorway, the attentive wanderer may perceive a coat of arms, well preserved, and hewn in stone, consisting of three shields; in the one he will see the lion of the Palatinate, in the other the chequers of Bavaria, and in the third, on a red ground, the branch or twig (in damask), upon which it is said, that the imperial globe or apple of the empire grew ripe, and above the crest of the coat of arms is an other lion saltant. At the bottom of the arms, the ground of which is still green, is seen the date of the building of this part of the castle in 1524. A winding staircase leads from the gothic doorway of the tower to the upper stories of this building.

To the south, the great kitchen and household depart-ments adjoin it; almost all these parts are in good pre-servation, and comprise up to the eastern angle hand-some dwelling apartments in two stories, the first floor of which is occupied as the castle tavern during the winter, and the second let to strangers during the summer.

The seignorial kitchen and confectionary department (*E. 1*) is, on account of its large hearth and chimney, worthy of attention.

Further to the left in the north wing we enter a rather spacious vault, which was said to have been the slaughter-house (*E. 2*) but now used for stabling, and again to the west, in the same building, we reach the former baking-house (*E. 3*) with its striking gigantic chimney.

As these buildings offer nothing more worthy of attention, I shall not describe them further, and only notice the projection on the south side, which strikes the eye of every visitor. This is the large well of the castle (*E. 4*), formerly 60 feet deep, under a portico, at that time vaulted over with gothic pointed arches, borne by four isolated and two wall-pillars. These four pillars and a part of the fifth, are of a grey, coarse-grained syenite, similar pieces whereof are to be found in these parts, [1] which has led many writers to believe they were of this country, and left upon this spot by the ancient Romans, having perhaps formerly served as ornaments to a temple; but more ancient writers, for example, the celebrated cosmographer and master of arts Sebastian Münster — who taught at Heidelberg in 1524 — had seen these pillars in his youth among the ruins of the palace of Charles the great at Ingelheim, to where this great Emperor had had a hundred similar pillars brought from Rome and Ravenna to decorate his imperial castle. The Elector Louis V. had these remaining pillars and three others [2] taken from the old imperial palace of Ingelheim, and brought to the electoral residence, where they still serve as the modest supporters to the projection which encloses the well, but they are

---

[1] In order to give explorers an opportunity of examining the similarity of this sort of stone, upon the spot, the editor of this work, has procured a large piece of the gigantic pillar near Reichenbach at the foot of the Melibocus; this fragment is deposited before that part of the castle inhabited by the castellain, near the arcade of the „New Yard", for the inspection of every stranger.

[2] One of these three pillars is in the GARDEN or SCHWETZINGEN, while the two others are to be seen in the garden of the RHEINLUST at MANNHEIM.

deprived of their former capitals. The celebrated Marquard Freher also relates the same facts upon this subject.

Not alone to Louis V. do we owe the building of this part of the castle, but it was he also, who from the plans of his father, the Elector Philip, caused the whole of the castle to be surrounded with immense fortifications, formed a subterranean line of communication from the so-called blown-up tower to that which he afterwards constructed, and after him called the Louis-Tower; in the XVIIth century it bore the name of Nimmerleer (Never-empty); he further erected the gigantic building of the great rampart, now called the Elisabethan Garden; he likewise built the large tower to the northwest, on the ruins of the Jetta-Chapel; another, (at present the octagon-tower), and the large watchtower to the south, which were all united by subterranean communications; but as these principal works afterwards, underwent other forms and destinations, they will be more largely described in the second wandering through the fortifications of the castle.

Louis V. received with right the name of the Pacific; for it was he, who in all the assemblies of the princes, tried to maintain the peace of Germany, in those stormy times (1532) when the different religious confessions not only disunited single families, but whole empires.

Under the portal of the large watch-tower, which he had erected out of the dreadful depth of the ditch, he one day received the Emperor Charles V., in whose mighty empire, it is said, the sun was never known to set, and his haughty son, Philip II. of Spain, whom he feasted for two days in Rupert's regal halls.

This pacific Elector died in 1544, without issue, and was buried in the church of the Holy Ghost. His brother Frederick II. succeeded him as Palsgrave and Elector, and gloriously finished the buildings commenced by his predecessor.

We refer our readers to the letter *C*, as well as to the following letters *F*, *G*, *H*, *J* which contain many more accounts of this distinguished prince.

F.

THE BRIDGE-HOUSE.

If the wanderer wishes to enter the court-yard of the castle on coming from the gardens, he must first pass under the Bridge-house, formerly a sort of little fort or tête de pont, which Louis V. caused to be erected before his beautiful bridge, and which he had surrounded by ditches and palisades; two draw-bridges conducted to it, a large one for pieces of ordnance, carriages etc., and a smaller one for foot-passengers. Instead of the larger one he had a stone bridge built, and the little draw-bridge which is drawn up, is still visible. This Bridge-house has been used in the course of time for many services, for some time it served as a school for the children of the garrison; a few years ago Mr. Charles de Graimberg used it for his Exhibition of Pictures, and now it is let to strangers as a summer residence. After having passed the archway of the Bridge-house, you arrive at the large bridge, where every visitor generally casts a look into the vast depth of the castle ditch, and still pays respect to the memory of Louis V. who founded these bold edifices.

Now immediately before him the wanderer will perceive

G.

THE LARGE QUADRANGULAR WATCH-TOWER,

which, like the three above-mentioned buildings, also owes its origin to Louis V. Strangers are often seen to amuse themselves by listening at the last groove of the outer arch towards the castle-yard, and by a singular acoustic effect, a person placing his ear at the other side, hears perfectly what the one opposite to him, utters in a low voice; and who, in the innocent years of his childhood, for the first time enters this splendid princely castle, does not remember the large iron ring, which is given to him to bite, in order to gain admittance into the castle? Oh! happy times, the golden days of childhood! with what different views will life and this place be regarded by him who returns as an old man, to revisit the castle, and at the sight of the iron ring compares the present times to those gone by, an interval of time, which to him perhaps has been an iron one, and sorrowfully casts a look upon the ring, the ruins and himself, he likewise having become a ruin of what he formerly was. For the bridge and watch-tower, I would request the wanderer to refer to the letters *ff* and *gg*, in the second wandering, where they are enumerated in the order of the fortifications.

The view from the watch-tower over the ruins, produces a singular impression, for you have a complete bird's eye view of the castle. The former dials of the clock were of metal, and were taken away by the French during the war of the Orleans succession.

You now enter through the square watch-tower into the principal court-yard, where your eye is every where struck with the ruins of the magnificence and grandeur of past times.

H.

THE BIG TOWER.

According to chronological order, we have now to make mention of the b i g tower, at one time one of the largest in Europe, for it was 235 feet high and more than 90 feet in diameter; but we must refer our readers to the description of the Elisabethan-garden, as well as the wanderings through the fortifications, where this immense tower is described. The seven stories of this tower rested upon springers, several of which the visitor may still see on examining the remains.

J.

THE NEW COURT.

It was under this name that Frederick II.[1]) in 1549 erected an edifice on the remains of some old buildings, which may have dated their existence from the time of the Romans.

He had all the stones and rubbish cleared away, and built the so-called „new court" over them.

Some chronologists are of opinion that the old J e t t a - C a s t l e, and later the S c h l i e r b u r g, were built upon

---

[1]) Frederick II. was allowed by the emperor Charles V. to wear the imperial orb in his arms, for the services he had rendered to that prince and the empire; so from that time this emblem may be seen in the arms of the Palatinate. The elector Frederick II. died at Alzey, and was buried in the church of the Holy-Ghost at Heidelberg. With this prince the Heidelberg line became extinct, and the Palatinate of Neuburg was invested with the electoral dignity.

this same spot over the remains of an old roman fort, the ruins of which Frederick had cleared away, and erected this edifice over them, which is to be recognised when standing in the castle-yard and looking towards the north, by the three rows of short bulky pillars lying over each other. Here are to be seen above the first row, three coats of arms, surrounded with wreaths, the first to the left bears the arms of Frederick II., the centre one those of the Palatinate, the last to the right the arms of Frederick the second's wife, and also the date of the year 1549.

In a large room (*I. 1*) of this building, the library existed, but it was afterwards converted into the electoral audit-office; a small octagon tower, like that further to the south, was likewise erected here, and which led to the upper apartments.

If the attentive wanderer will follow me into the vaults of this edifice (*I. 2*), he will still see the interesting spot, where the chapel of the prophetess Jetta is once said to have stood. A little opening, which is now smaller, and formerly of the length of a man, forms a passage from the ground floor into this vault, through the centre of the ceiling, and furnishes to the observer rich materials for reflection upon its primitive destination. Some old walls of the remotest times are plainly to be seen here.

This vault, which we shall call the „Jetta-vault", both on account of its antiquity and by the singularity of its construction, is in my opinion the most interesting part of the whole subterranean part of the castle. The floor of this vault and some of the lower walls are of a lively granite.

The openings towards the palace of OTHO-HENRY prove that this „New-court", formerly stood alone, and it appears strange to the observer, that the staircase hewn out of the granite flooring, is constructed in such a manner, that though the light-holes of the vault are seen from all sides, yet still the staircase remains in complete obscurity. The whole of this magnificent vault, as well as the staircase which was formerly closed by a trap-door, and the corridor communicating with the octagon tower were all filled up with rubbish, which I had cleared away and thereby rendered them accessible. It is 13 feet high, 26 feet broad and 89 feet long. Like the staircase hewn out of the granite, and communicating to the octagon tower, another staircase opposite to this, led to the aforementioned little octagon tower, with the winding staircase, and from this to the three galleries that are seen from the court yard; on the second gallery of which, the wife of the elector CHARLES LOUIS in 1657 [1]), was about to shoot with a pistol Mademoiselle de Degenfeld, of whom she was jealous, but was prevented by the presence of mind of the chamberlain count Wolf Julius of Hohenlohe, who snatched the weapon from her hand, and fired it in the air.

A little dark vault near to the large one, abovementioned is also interesting, for there is a small opening in it, its real destination is likewise very mysterious, and furnishes a subject of enquiry to the antiquary.

In the thirty years war this building was burnt to the walls; CHARLES LOUIS had it restored again; but in the war of the Orleans' succession it was again destroyed by the French, and though renewed by CHARLES PHILIP in 1718, it again became a prey to the flames at the great fire of the castle in 1764.

Which of our readers, on contemplating these burnt

---

[1]) In 1657 elector Charles Louis separated from his wife, Charlotte, princess of Hessen-Cassel, and married with the left hand, Mademoiselle Maria Louisa of Degenfeld-Dürnau and Neuhausen, daughter of general Baron Martin of Degenfeld, at the castle of Schwetzingen, whereby she was raised to the rank of a raugravine.

walls, does not remember a stanza from the Bell of the great poet Schiller, in which he says:

Leer gebrannt	Waste is now
Ist die Stätte	The place and dread,
Wilder Stürme rauhes Bette.	Of wild storms the rugged bed.
In den öden Fensterhöhlen	In the hollow window cells
Wohnt das Grauen	Horror dwells,
Und des Himmels Wolken schauen	And the clouds from Heaven's sphere
Hoch hinein.	Downwards peer.

(A. Baskerville's Translation.)

In this building there was a manufactory of tapestry (worked carpets, Gobelins) also celebrated at that period, but entirely destroyed by the lightning, which struck the edifice and set it on fire. This part of the castle now forms a very picturesque view, particularly towards the east, where, on the second floor, there is a very elegant balcony in the gothic style. — The large arched buttress on the north side was built after the second fire, in order to support the edifice which was very much shaken, and threatened to give way; apartments were also erected in it. The building in the front, in the shape of a tower, which is to be recognised from the castle yard by its sun-dial, was also built by Frederick II., and served for the dwelling of the Castellain. Below is a large gate, which at that time was the principal entrance to the arsenal, now entirely destroyed. At the present day this building forms a part of the Castellain's dwelling.

K.

THE OCTAGON-TOWER.

The foundations of this tower (*K. 1*) seem to be of a very primitive origin, and the old staircase hewn out of granite, which leads from the Jetta-vault, to the vaults of this tower, announce a more ancient origin than that of the foundations, namely the fortifications constructed by FREDERICK THE VICTORIOUS, LOUIS V. and FREDERICK II. The lowest foundations of the tower, like those of the arsenal, are perhaps the remains of a former period.

On the top of this tower, as far as we perceive it is round, was a high pointed roof, which Frederick II. had removed, and placed on the under-structure, now the so-called octagon-tower with the high bay-windows. It is interesting to know, that the subterranean vault of this tower is without a central pillar, while all the upper departments which rest upon it, have each in their centre a strong square pillar, five feet in diameter, and consequently all this line of pillars has no other foundation than the vault without a pillar whereby we may easily judge of the solidity of the edifice.

On this lower vault, there is also another in two compartments (*K. 2*); by means of the winding staircase in the little round tower built to the west, you may reach it, the interior of which is surrounded by loop-holes, and like the other part served as a fortification.

The large pillar, and the eight pillars which surround it, and pass through two of the stories, were placed here by Frederick II., in order to give more solidity to the octagon building.

The first story in the octagon building (*K. 3*), was a large open room, surrounded by a gallery from without. Frederick II. had a bell cast in 1550, and suspended it in this story, from which the tower was afterwards called „THE BELFRY." In 1551, when the elector was returning to his residence from a journey in Lorraine, his ear was struck for the first time with the beautiful sound of this bell on Corpus-Christi day.

Frederick IV. later had the roof taken off in 1608, added a story to it, with a second gallery, and covered this new building with a roof in the form of a dome, so that this tower at present consists of six stories. In the thirty-years' war 1633, the Swedes damaged this building very much, so that CHARLES LOUIS had it restored and newly roofed; but already in 1689, the French tried to undermine it, the traces of three attempts may still be seen in the lower vault. They set fire to the supporters of the roof, so that in 1718 it received a new roof; in 1764, the lightning struck the adjoining „New-court", which caused this tower to take fire, and the large bell was melted; since when, the tower has remained in its actual state. A new wooden gallery leads from the „New-court" to this tower, so interesting from its charming prospect and interesting appearance; it is ascended without difficulty to the extreme top, and where the winding staircases cease or are demolished, their places have now been filled up with wooden steps.

L.

THE LIBRARY-TOWER.

Behind the Louis-building, FREDERICK II. caused a round tower, furnished with a quantity of windows, to be erected on the foundations built by FREDERICK II., and according to Dr Leger, placed his library there, wherefore it is called the library-tower, and from the dispensary being established there, it also received the name of the apothecary's tower.

In the lower part of this edifice towards the east, are again to be seen the arms of the wife of FREDERICK II.;

but these walls are of prior origin, therefore it is to be concluded, that when this elector completed the upper building, he caused these arms to be likewise placed on the older lower building.

Other writers in contradiction to Leger, maintain that FREDERICK IV. first built this upper story and had it turned into a library.

This tower was also destroyed in the thirty-years' war, and like the afore mentioned building restored by CHARLES LOUIS, but likewise damaged in the war of the Orleans' succession, and again repaired by CHARLES PHILIP and inhabited till 1764, when it became a prey to the flames, like the most part of the buildings to the north and east of the castle.

FREDERICK II. to whom our castle owes so many new creations, and also highly honored by his emperor, for his services as we have mentioned before — was authorised to bear the imperial orb in his arms, and which has ever since appeared in the escutcheon of the electors Palatine.

After the death of Frederick II. at Alzey, his cousin OTHO-HENRY surnamed the Magnanimous, ascended the throne of the Palatinate.

To him we owe the most magnificent and perfect monument of art in the whole castle, which I will describe in the following notice.

The winding staircase of the library-tower, in perfect good preservation, and which by exception is found in the interior, and not in an adjoining tower like in most of the other structures, leads through the Louis-building to the first story of the palace of OTHO-HENRY.

———

M.

THE OTHO - HENRY - BUILDING.

The plan of this edifice, so perfect in all its proportions, and which in its ruins presents to the eye such a delightful spectacle, is said to be attributed — by many high authorities in art — to the most celebrated painter, sculptor and architect of his age, Michael Angelo, and if it were so, it is certain it would not disgrace that great artist; but though that great master has planned and executed many buildings of this kind, the architect of the OTHO - HENRY - palace, was a native of Heidelberg, who during the delineation of his plan, may very probably have had in his mind the works of the great Italian. [1] This building was commenced in the year 1556; it presents itself in all its parts in perfect harmony, and though the eye is everywhere assailed with an infinite richness of sculpture and of statues, it is never disturbed by tasteless profusion or insipid deficiency of art.

OTHO HENRY was the last elector of the old Heidelberg electoral line and a great protector of the arts; his great affection for them gained for him from his contemporaries, the surname of the „Magnanimous.‟

The monument which this august prince left to posterity, even in the ruins of his magnificent palace, is to day a proof how liberally he protected and cultivated the arts. Assuredly we cannot behold the splendour of the façade of this building, almost in a perfect state of preservation, without exalted admiration, and proclaiming it to be a model of the highest perfection of the roman-italian

---

[1] His name is said to have been BOOHER, or as it was called in italian BOOHARIO; the four caryatides on the gate are likewise supposed to be his work; but the other figures were finished by less skilful artists.

style. The visitor must become enchanted with the inexhaustible originality, the symetry which pervades in all the parts of this sumptuous building, the pure taste in the order and proportions of the windows, with the various effects of the haut-and bas-reliefs, as well as with the richness of the figures, arabesques, forms of the plants, arms and the attributes of agriculture; what is particularly to be noticed is the exquisitely finished work of the drapery of the four statues which support the entablature of the grand portal with its ornaments.

Over the arch of the portal the following words are inscribed in german:

„Otto Heinrich von Gottes Gnaden, Pfalzgraf bei Rhein, des heiligen römischen Reichs Erztruchses und Churfürst Herzog in Nieder- und Ober-Bayern etc."

„Otho Henry by the grace of God, palsgrave of the Rhine, arch-dapifer and elector of the holy roman empire, Duke of Lower- and Upper-Bavaria etc."

and above this inscription are the arms of the founder, a perfect chef-d'œuvre of sculpture; on both sides of the arms are figures fighting with lions, representing an allegory of the wars that the electoral house had experienced in the course of time; the most elevated part of the portal is ornamented with the bust of the founder. The figures of the first story designate together strength and dexterity, which ought to serve as a basis to all works — from the left to the right — JOSHUA, SAMPSON, HERCULES and DAVID; the figures of the second story show the five christian virtues: patience, faith, charity, hope and justice. — The spirited inventor of the plan wished to express by these symbolical figures, that these virtues might continue to adorn the princes of the noble house of WITTELSBACH, and if they possessed those precious qualities, the master would also promise them temporal pleasures — they should enjoy the pleasures of the chase (Diana), the commerce of

PORTAL DES OTT

the country would flourish (Mercury), love would make them happy (Venus); war would spare their country, and come out victorious (Mars) and time (Saturn) would bless them in the upper and lower world (Jupiter) and (Vulcan); the first five pagan deities which these allegories express ornament the third story, and the two last the pediments.

On the upper row of all are three lions, each holding the arms of the Palatinate.

Near the raised pediments of the first row of windows, we perceive heads in the form of medallions, which represent great and illustrious Romans.

The vaults (*M. 1*), several of which in my opinion are still filled with rubbish, were magazines for the preservation of stores.

A double staircase, formerly ornamented with a magnificent iron balustrade, that was sold at a great loss in the eighteenth century, leads to the beautiful portico, and from this to a short corridor (*M. 2*), the three doors of which are beautifully ornamented with arabesques.

On going through the door in face of the portal you reach a large entrance hall (*M. 3*), the doors of which are likewise distinguished by their magnificent haut- and bas-reliefs; the visitor of refined taste will be sadly shocked, when he enters these venerable halls, and beholds the wanton injuries and vile disfigurements of many of these sculptures, and must agree in the opinion of the late Dr Leger, who in his guide says: „What a pity it is, that these master-pieces of the chisel, these models of the art of drawing, should every where be so disfigured by premeditated marks of depredation. It is our duty to be true to history and to truth! neither the Swede in the thirty-years' war, nor the Frenchman under the administration of Louvois, have indignantly profaned these treasures of art. It is the disregard for antiquity and art, which in great measure our contemporaries possess, and the wantonness of the unrestrained lower classes who, here united, have left behind them a monument of their genius and their civilization."

These important words of a man so distinguished by his knowledge of art and antiquity, may perhaps have been the cause, that in order to prevent any further marks of injury being committed, these magnificent ruins have been closed to the public by order of the government, and can only be opened under the conduct of the guides.

The well-known scientific men and artists of Heidelberg and the neighbourhood who desire to see the palace of Otho-Henry, solely for interests of art or business, will be amply remunerated for their trouble by applying for entrance to the Castellain, who will readily grant it to them, he being well convinced, that no impure hand will here dare to exercise its malice.

But let us now enter to the left, by a doorway ornamented in the same exquisite taste as the rest, into the throne room, afterwards called the „emperors' hall" (*M. 4*), now falsely termed the „knights' hall." Here is plainly to be seen, without a stretch of imagination, the place where the throne stood, in a deeply raised niche between two Ionic columns (*M. 5*); to what purpose the two little concealed spaces on both sides of the throne were used, I leave to the penetrating imagination of the architect and antiquary who may visit these ruins to explain.

It was in this hall in 1562, on the emperor MAXIMILIAN THE SECOND'S return from his coronation at Francfort, that he was sumptuously entertained, and where, when he again honored the castle of Heidelberg in 1570, with a visit to FREDERICK III., the successor of OTHO HENRY, he was dreadfully frightened by a lion. — Most of the counts Palatine kept tame lions as living emblems of their rhenish duchy, and FREDERICK III. was in the habit of feeding his lion during dinner with his own hand; it was in this hall when suddenly the door opened, the king of the beasts entered and sprung upon the emperor, who was sitting at table in the usual seat of the elector, thinking it was his own master. Naturally the illustrious guest was not a little frightened nor did he recover himself, till the elector called the royal animal to his side.

From the time of this imperial visit, this room was called the „emperor's hall." This splendid throne room or emperor's hall, was formerly covered with beautiful crossed vaultings, supported by two columns with costly carvings, some of the remains of wich have been now brought back to their former place of destination. The door-frames of the hall and those of the other splendid apartments of this story, are of a fine yellow sand-stone from Heilbronn, ornamented as we have before descri-bed, with a variety of caryatides, genii, trophies, fruits, flowers and foliage; all these divers ornaments are often copied by artists.

The other apartments to the west (*M. 6*), were used as drawing-rooms, and the room to the side towards the east (*M. 7*) which adjoins the library-tower, was used by the officers in waiting.

The halls and apartments of the upper stories (*M. 8*) were decorated in the most sumptuous manner of the times, and served as state-rooms on grand festival oc-casions, or as dwellings for the illustrious visitors at the castle. It was in these upper appartments that the lover of the arts, CHARLES THEODORE, according to the accounts of both eye- and ear-witnesses [1]), had formed the resolution to retransfer his residence to Hei-

---

[1]) The Castellain Cramer, the steward of the castle Auth and the court-butler Verhass.

delberg, every thing was prepared for the sumptuous furnishing of the castle, the court already equipped for its return to the old electoral seat, when the lightning struck the „New-court" built by FREDERICK II., set it on fire, and the whole of the edifice as well as the magnificent buildings adjoining, with a great quantity of the superbly embroidered tapestry became a prey to the flames caused by the lightning, and were burnt to the walls; the pious-minded CHARLES THEODORE and his consort ELISABETH AUGUSTA saw in this event a warning of providence, and the restoration of the castle has been discontinued from that day.

By a staircase (*M. 9*) constructed in the library-tower, you may reach through the Louis-building, those upper parts of this edifice which are accessible.

OTHO HENRY, the last scion of the old Heidelberg electoral line only reigned three years, and died already in 1559, and was interred in the vault of his ancestors in the church of the holy ghost; the line of Simmern succeeded him in the electoral dignity. Before the lightning had destroyed the interior of this building, it had suffered much by the flames of the thirty-years' war and that of the Orléans' succession; and what was then spared, fell by degrees into decay, through the ignorance of certain functionaries employed afterwards, and as we have said before, by the brutal hand of the lower order of the people. But the present age will take care that this magnificent ruin be preserved for posterity. The visitor will observe in the yard, a wall which extends before the Otho-Henry-building and that of Louis V.; this was constructed by the architect in order to conceal from view the declivity of the ground; we shall however return to this, in describing more fully the beautiful buildings of FREDERICK IV.

FREDERICK III. was the first scion of the line of Simmern who occupied the throne of the electoral Palatinate;

he was only known by his contemporaries and brethren in the faith, by the name of the „Pious“; he married MARY OF BRANDENBURG, reigned 17 years, and left no monuments of architecture; he died in 1576 and was buried in the church of the Holy Ghost. His son LOUIS VI. succeeded him in the government, and married Anne of East-Friesland, but a few years afterwards he died in 1583, leaving behind him a son under age; he also lies near the remains of his pious father in the church of the Holy Ghost.

JOHN CASIMIR, brother of the deceased elector, undertook the guardianship of the minor, and it is to this chivalrous prince that we owe the construction of the first great Tun, a more detailed description of which we shall give in the following section.

N.

THE GREAT TUN.

In Heidelberg beim grossen Fass
Da liess sich's fröhlich sein.
Bei einem vollgefüllten Glas
Von edlem Pfälzer Wein;
Denn als dies Fass kam einst zu Stand
Da war ein Jubel in dem Land,
Da freut' sich Alles, Gross und Klein,
Denn voll war es mit Pfälzer Wein. [1])
Richard Wanderer.

How beautiful thou shinest Heidelberg, how superb thy surrounding country looks adorned with the charms

----

[1]) In Heidelberg, the „Grosse Fass“
Caused merry days to shine,
When all enjoyed the well fill'd glass,
Of noble Pfälzer wine;

4

50

of spring, of summer and of autumn, far and wide renowned is thy university, which the first Rupert built within thy walls; but it is not thy charm, O animating nature, which for centuries has spread abroad the glory of this town; not alone the pearl of science that attracts the pilgrim from the remotest lands; but the altar that is erected here to the jovial God „Bacchus" in the far famed „Great Tun" this colossal altar, that draws pilgrims from the north, south, east and west, to view in silent admiration this giant of all tuns, and on returning to their distant homes, for years after, relate to their children and grand-children an account of this wonderful master-piece.

The Count Palatine John Casimir, the guardian of his nephew, and who undertook the administration of the Palatinate at the death of his brother the Elector Louis VI., was an excellent prince, a courageous soldier, a jovial and happy man, who in 1589, when the vines produced such an abundancy of grapes, that all over the country where vineyards were to be found, the joy was universal, conceived the idea of constructing this great tun, which for times immemorial was to announce to posterity the riches of that blessed year. It was thus, under this great prince, that the grand sign of Heidelberg, „the Great Tun" was built, but first of all the building in which it reposes.

When you are upon the balcony, which we shall describe in the following section, you will see to your left a building with a large lion's head, which the Count Palatine John Casimir added to the Rupertina-chapel, and now conceals in its cellar, this celebrated sign of

For when this Tun first came to light,
All did in joy combine
To see the „Fass", oh wondrous sight!
Fill'd up with Pfälzer wine.

Das

GROSSE FASS

im

LE | THE
GRAND TONNEAU | GREAT TUN IN

CHÂTEAU | Schloss | THE CASTLE

| | zu | OF

Heidelberg

Heidelberg, that every traveller must see on visiting this town, for having been to Heidelberg without having seen the „Great Tun", is become as proverbial as „having been to Rome without having seen the Pope". In the first years of my youth, I travelled a great deal, but little was then heard abroad of the beautiful surrounding country of Heidelberg, very little of its university, the oldest however of Germany, and which has produced many distinguished statesmen and learned men; but in the remotest lands, this gigantic tun was known and spoken of, and that it contained nearly t h r e e h u n d r e d t h o u s a n d bottles of wine in its huge compass.

The blessings which were poured down on the prosperity of the vines towards the end of the sixteenth century, must, as already observed, have determined JOHN CASIMIR, Count Palatine of the Rhine, and Duke of Bavaria, great as a prince and benevolent as a man, on constructing this tun of all tuns, which posterity was to admire.

He therefore sent for MICHAEL WERNER the most experienced cooper in his trade, from the free city of Landau, and caused him to build a tun, second to none in size in the whole world, and to erect it in the vault of the newly constructed building, that John Casimir had adjoinced to the Rupertina-chapel.

Five lions couchant ornamented this tun, the largest of them on the top of the front side, and the smaller ones at the corners, each bearing the arms of the Palatinate.

In the year 1589 the work was begun, and in 1591 Master WERNER finished his task to the perfect satisfaction of the prince. This first and oldest great tun was placed on the same spot where the present tun is now to be seen, and contained 132 fuders, 3 ohms and 3 quarter-casks or nearly 133,000 quarts of wine. It was 27 feet long, had 112 staves bound with 24 iron hoops, for which 122 hundred weight of iron is said to have been used. The master-cooper received fl. 1500 for his work, and the locksmith fl. 1400.

But this giant tun was not destined long to continue the delight of its founder and its visitors; for a year after its construction JOHN CASIMIR died, and in the thirty-years' war it was demolished after an existence of scarcely thirty years, and lay neglected and almost forgotten in its ruined state for upwards of forty years; it was not for a long time after the calamities of this fatal war, when the golden peace began again to flourish, and to show the blessed fruits of the increasing prosperity of the people, that the Count Palatine and Elector CHARLES LOUIS, in 1664, repaired the castle of Heidelberg, as far as it lay in his power, in order to remove all the traces which this cruel war had left behind, and caused another new great tun, as a remembrance of the returning cheerfulness of the people, to be constructed by the electoral state-cooper JOHN MEIER whom he ordered to build it with greater skill and splendour; and this second great tun was larger than the former, it being now 24 feet high, and 30 feet long; it contained 204 fuders (nearly 238,000 quarts) and like the first was bound with 24 hoops, but far exceeding it in splendour and richness of workmanship.

But unfortunately this great tun was also not long the object of general admiration, for the claims of succession of the house of Orleans again spread the flames of war over the Palatinate, this cherished land of nature, and threatened not only the tun but the whole castle with total ruin.

It is only too well known, that towards the end of the XVIIth century, in the years 1689 and 1693, with what hatred the french troops ravaged the beautiful Palatinate, and with what rage, unworthy of a civilized nation, they burned and ransacked those smiling villages and flourishing towns, and crowned their misdeeds by the destruction of the castle of Heidelberg; it is true that by chance the tun escaped the destructive fury of the french soldiers and the flames they spread all around; still in these disastrous times of war, the necessary care could not be taken of it, so it lay 41 years empty, it sprung in several places and was spoilt; but when under the Elector Palatine Charles Philip, the castle was restored as much as possible, he thought of this mouldering gigantic tun, ordered it to be renewed and richly ornamented.

Now this work was begun under the inspection of the court-cooper JOHN ANTHONY ENGLER in 1727 and fortunately completed in the following year, when it was filled with wine of the Palatinate. It was near this tun that the statue of Clement Perkeo (N. 2) was erected, and which still exists; he was called CLEMENTEL (the diminutive of Clement), on account of his dwarfish figure, and enjoyed a widely spread reputation at that time by his merry and witty conceits, as court-fool to the Elector Palatine CHARLES PHILIP.

This Clementel was a Tyrolese by birth, and formerly a button-maker; he was exercising his trade when the Elector first became acquainted with him during his sojourn in Tyrol, as imperial governor of that country, and attached him to his court as „merry counsellor" or buffoon. It was this merry counsellor, who, being a great and zealous votary of the juice of the grape, persisted so long with the Elector, till the latter in the year 1727, resolved upon restoring this king of all tuns, and appointed Clementel chamberlain to the royal vat, to which distinction, according to all reports still extant, he endeavoured to do all honour, by drinking daily from 15 to 18 bottles of its good wine.

Mr. A. VON LEONHARD in his excellent Heidelberg-guide relates the following anecdote of this buffoon:

Perkeo was however said to be a man of education, and the Elector generally admitted him to his table. One day, the minister of CHARLES PHILIP, a man of a very tall figure, teazed the dwarf, and ended with these words: „Come near to me, Perkeo, and give me a kiss; but don't stretch yourself". The answer of the dwarf, on making a very profound bow, was the same, which the knight with the iron hand (Götz von Berlichingen) sent by his trumpeter to the imperial captain, with this addition: „but without stooping".

At the side of Clementel, there is a clock (*N. 3*), the mechanism of which is said to be an invention of this merry fool, and surprises those who wind it up in a very pleasant manner.

This tun also soon became useless, and its profuse ornaments and antiquated verses, universally displeased; therefore the Elector CHARLES THEODORE, in order to respect the foundation of his ancestors, resolved to have another tun made, which was to surpass in size all the former ones, so in 1751 he ordered his court-cooper, JOHN JACOB ENGLER the younger, to construct a new tun of the best wood, and it is this one, respected wanderer, that you still see to-day, and which attracts pilgrims from far and near, to view its gigantic construction.

This chief of all the tuns in the world, is said to have cost the enormous sum of 80,000 florins, and was often filled with the costly wine of the Palatinate; it is 32 feet long, 22 feet in diameter at both ends, and 23 feet in the centre. Its 127 staves are $9\frac{3}{4}$ inches thick, and its circular bung-hole from 3 to 4 inches in diameter; eighteen wooden hoops — 8 inches thick and 15 inches broad — the different rafters of which are bound together with iron hoops and screws, but the hoops at the two extremities, are 18 inches in breadth. Of the hoops that now remain, there are only eight, and it is not known up to the present day, how they have disappeared. From the front as well as the back ends of the tun, bent in towards the interior to meet the pressure of the liquid, it is each time held in towards the centre in its concave form, by four strong rafters, the ends of which are fastened to the bottom and to the staves by iron hoops and screws.

The tun reposes upon 8 very strong wooden supporters, beautifully carved, and raised several feet from the ground.

The height of the whole work is from the floor of the cellar to its highest point 26 feet 5 inches, and on the top in the front, there is a shield surmounted with the electoral cap on an azure field, the initials in gold of CHARLES THEODORE. This mighty tun surpasses in size all its predecessors, for it can contain 236 fuders or 283,000 large bottles of fluid in its colossal space, and which as before observed, has often (1753, 1760 and 1766) been completely filled with the wine of the Palatinate.

There are still to be seen in the cellar, the compasses, plane, gouge and timber-mark (N. 4), which were used for its construction. The large compasses are 8 feet 6 inches long, on which some verses are carved; the plane is 7 feet long, $10^3/_4$ inches broad and $4^1/_2$ inches thick, with the name of the head-workman engraved on it.

A gallery with railings and staircases leads all round and to the top of this gigantic tun, over which a flooring, or so called balcony, is constructed, 27 feet 7 inches above the floor of the cellar, where a numerous company may assemble to enjoy the pleasure of the dance, and surrounded with a railing 3 feet 3 inches high.

This vat is filled by a vertical opening in the top of the vault, and the whole cellar to the roof is 35 feet

3 inches high; there is also a little iron pump over the cellar, by which the tun may be emptied.

Before this huge tun, a smaller one of ordinary dimensions is placed by way of contrast (*N. 5*), which is remarkable on account of its being made without hoops, and strongly put together without any visible fastening, in the most artistical manner.

We will add to our little work a faithful engraving of this large tun, and hope that the visitor of Heidelberg will, in seeing its effigy before him, preserve a faithful remembrance of our giant.

The usual entrance (*N. 6*) to the cellar which contains the tun — (there are however still two more) — leads through the large cellar of the cooperage, where there is likewise a second large tun, that was built in 1662, consisting of 94 staves, and holding 47 fuders; in the time of its splendour this cellar is said to have contained 12 similar casks; also another cask (*N. 7*), of ordinary size, bound with iron hoops and appearing to be very ancient, the front of which is surmounted with an image of the Madonna, cut in oak; this cask is said to have contained the sacramental wine.

The building in which our giant-tun is placed, consists of three compartments; the lower vault communicated with the fortifications, and over this vault, the one which contains the tun (these two compartments corresponded by means of a trap-door) and above the whole, was a little chapel used for family devotion, the large gothic windows of which are still visible, but in a dilapidated state. From the large chapel one could enter the smaller one, communicating to it by a large gothic arched door; Frederick V. united this edifice with the english palace, which we shall mention hereafter, and erected a balcony upon it. This building was destroyed in 1689, but was newly roofed in 1728.

O.

THE FREDERICK'S-BUILDING.

After the death of John Casimir in 1592, his nephew Frederick IV., son of Louis VI., succeeded to the government; a written diary of his from the 9th January 1596 to the 26th January 1599 is still preserved in the Library of the University of Heidelberg. In this prince, that taste for architecture again survived, which, for the most part, had animated the princes of the line of Heidelberg.

It was this prince, who in 1606, founded the town of Mannheim, which afterwards became so dangerous to its eldest sister on the banks of the Neckar; and on the Jettabühl he erected a new palace, though built in a heavy style, and which towers in a proud and lordly manner over Heidelberg. The foundation stone of this pompous but overcharged building was laid in 1601 and the edifice completed in 1607. It is built in three stories, surmounted with gable-ends on the north and south-sides, ornamented with figures with cornucopias and birds, probably an allusion to the richness of the country which ever shines in juvenile plenitude. In each gable are to be seen two shields, the arms of the Elector Frederick IV., and his wife the princess Louise of Orange-Nassau; between the gables over two frontispieces, stands the figure of Justice with the sword and balance, and from the side, looking into the Court-yard, you will perceive 16 well carved statues (in each story four), representing all the distinguished princes of the house of Wittelsbach.

Over the door through which you enter the building, there is a tablet, which was damaged during the Swedish wars, bearing the following inscription:

FRIDERICUS COMES PALATINUS RHENI S. ROM. IMPERII ELECTOR DUX BAVARIAE HOC PALATIUM DIVINO CULTUI ET COMMODAE HABITATIONI EXTRUENDUM ET MAJORUM SUORUM IMAGINIBUS EXORNANDUM CURAVIT. ANNO DOM. MDCVII.[1])

The first of these statues to the left in the gable at the top, is CHARLEMAGNE, the founder of the Christian-German Empire, from whom the ancient line of the Schyres or Wittelsbach, derives its extraction. The second is OTHO, the Great, Duke of Bavaria; the third LOUIS I., Palsgrave of the Rhine and Duke of Bavaria; the fourth RUDOLPH I. Palsgrave, Elector and founder of the Rudolph's building; the fifth Emperor LOUIS IV., the Bavarian, Rudolph's brother; the sixth RUPERT, as Elector RUPERT III., grandson of RUDOLPH and founder of the Rupert's building; the seventh OTHO, King of Hungary, Palsgrave of the Rhine, and grandson of OTHO, the Illustrious; the eighth CHRISTOPHER III., King of Denmark, Norway and Sweden, a grandson of King RUPERT; the ninth Palsgrave RUPERT I., Rudolph's son; the tenth FREDERICK I., the Victorious; the eleventh the Palsgrave and Elector FREDERICK II., the Wise, who completed the fortifications of the castle and built the New-court; the twelfth OTHO-HENRY, the Magnanimous, and the founder of the most beautiful building, which bears his name, and will ever remain a glorious monument of his refined taste; the thirteenth the Palsgrave and Elector FREDERICK III., the Pious, of the house of Palatine-Simmern; the fourteenth the Palsgrave and Elector LOUIS VI., son of the preceding named prince; the fifteenth Palsgrave JOHN CASIMIR, his brother and

---

[1]) „Frederic, Count Palatine of the Rhine, Elector of the holy Roman Empire, Duke of Bavaria, caused this palace to be constructed for divine service and commodious habitation, and ornamented it with the statues of his Ancestors; in the year of our Lord 1607."

Lieutenant of the Electorate; the sixteenth and last the Palsgrave and Elector FREDERICK IV., the builder of this pompous edifice. [1])

Unfortunately many of these statues have been damaged by the fury of the wars, particularly that of the eleventh, Elector FREDERICK II., the whole of the upper part of the body being carried away by a cannon-ball, and the fifteenth statue of JOHN CASIMIR, the upper part of which is likewise much damaged.

The ground floor and upper parts are occupied by the church, to which the treasures and charitable foundations of the Rupertina-chapel were removed, having partly been taken away, and partly appropriated to other uses. Over the principal entrance to the church, which like the whole building is not constructed in the purest style, is to be seen, inscribed in the hebrew and latin languages, the 20th verse of the 118th psalm:

"This is the gate of the Lord: the righteous shall enter into it."

It is interesting for the historian to find in the documents still extant, how the luxurious Frederick IV. long endeavoured in vain to procure a skilful artist for the execution of the sculptures for his palace, till at last he found one master Sebastian Götz of Chur in the Grisons, whom he immediately charged with the undertaking, together with 8 other workmen, on condition that the sculptuary work should be completed in one year, for which he was to receive for himself and his eight journeymen in ready money:

1) For each of the statues of the 16 ancestors of the electoral founder . . . . 65 fl.
2) For each of the four coats of arms on both sides of the four gable-ends. . , ... 40 fl.

---

[1]) Engravings of these venerable figures have been executed and designed by Mr. de Graimberg, of whom they can be purchased.

3) For each of the two statues of justice between
   the gable-ends. . . . . 30 fl.
4) For each of the 12 large lion's heads . . .   9 fl.
5) For each of the 3 small lion's heads . . .   3 fl.
6) For each of the 45 human heads over the
   windows, roofs and niches of the ancestral
   statues . . . .   3 fl.

The royal-hall — now the cellerage — was to be
arranged as a work-shop, to be heated during the
winter, and the master and his journeymen are said to
have during this time freely partaken of the good cheer
of the kitchen and cellar of the Elector-Palatine. The
sum also which master Götz received from the electoral
treasury was, for that time, very considerable, for
the materials, the Heilbronn yellow sandstone, and the
other requisites, were obliged to be delivered to him
free of expense.

The contract with the master was drawn up in 1604
and the year after, the honest Grison, with his journeymen, completed the work to the perfect satisfaction
of his august patron.

On examining this colossal work, it must be con-
fessed, that the sculptor and his men must have exer-
cised their chisel in a most masterly manner, to have
produced those beautiful creations in the short space
of one year. Besides the above enumerated objects,
there were many other things to be carried out in this
building which are not mentioned in our work, such as,
the four figures standing on the gable-ends, the shields
richly carved with ornaments on both sides of the pillars,
as well as the arms over the doors, framed in arabesques, with many others.

In proportion to the salaries compared with that
time and the present when a professor of our university
only got from 80 to 100 florins per annum, one may

conclude, from what master Götz and his journeymen received, that the fine arts in those days were not at all neglected. *Suum cuique!*

In the second story of this edifice M. Charles de Graimberg has preserved his choice collections of pictures, archives and antiquities, which principally relate to the history of the Palatinate, and contain above 2000 pictures, 900 manuscripts, 2000 engravings, old wood-cuts, 200 coins, 1200 deeds on parchment, and above 1000 specimens of figures of all description, old vases, house-utensils and arms. M. Charles de Graimberg has likewise published a rich collection of all the imaginable views of Heidelberg castle, drawn by himself, whereof the most celebrated are those engraved by Haldenwang, and which excellent engravings have not a little contributed to the numerous visits of strangers to Heidelberg up to this day. These views, as well as others relating to the ruins of the castle, are exposed for sale in a particular room of his gallery; and Mr. L. Meder the print-seller, also occupies a room on this floor, in which some most excellent pencillings, aquarels, paintings, engravings, lithographies and photographies of the most distinguished artists of the modern school are likewise offered for sale, so that strangers may procure remembrances of their visit in the castle itself.

The third story has up to this time no fixed destination.

On the north side of this sumptuous palace, the Elector Frederick IV. caused a beautiful balcony to be built upon the remains of the old wall of the castle, from whence the visitor can still enjoy a magnificent view over the town and the vast valley of the Rhine to the far distant mountains of the Haardt; this balcony is built upon strong vaults, supported by doric columns, the upper part of which is called the grand porch of the castle; the other parts contiguous to the balcony belonging to the fortifications of the castle, we shall describe in the wanderings through those parts.

In its style the Frederick's-building may be called pompous, but never beautiful, for a great deal of pomp has been lavished upon it, but the vast and heavy profusion of ornaments and scrolls, offend the eye in regard to beauty.

The church is only slightly injured, and could be repaired at a little expence.

A painting which was formerly over the high altar, representing St. John the Baptist, is very old; it was painted by Schoon Jans, born in Antwerp 1655, and bought by the Elector CHARLES, who had it placed in the church of the castle. It is one of those interesting memorials of antiquity of the middle age, which has been preserved by the vicissitudes of the times; its position over the high altar of the church now mourns for its lost ornament, for it has been actually carried away to the grand ducal gallery of paintings at Mannheim; the paintings which are still remaining in this church are of no value.

Under this church, there is a beautiful strong vault used as a cellar.

During the construction of this pompous work, the Elector FREDERICK IV. ornamented the court-yard of the castle with the large fountain (O. I.), the ruins of which the wanderer may still perceive. The late Grand-Duke LEOPOLD, a great admirer of all that is noble and sublime, on his visits to the castle of Heidelberg, has often been heard to express his wish that this large fountain should be restored, in order to revive the interior court-yard of these ruins; and this illustrious prince would really have fulfilled that wish, if the sad events of the times and his death had not prevented its realisation. May the worthy heir of his virtues and his throne respect this wish, in the accomplishment of it.

The declivity of the ground which hangs from the south-east corner of the yard towards the west and the north, is concealed by a beautiful free-stone wall, at the north end of which formerly stood the statue of Mercury, found at Neuenheim near Heidelberg; and likewise an antique roman altar dedicated to this god and dug up between Rohrbach and Kirchheim was placed below it; above the wall was another altar ornamented with inscriptions and images, and according to the inscriptions, dedicated by two brothers to Jupiter; the pedestal of this latter antiquity is still to be seen, and served for a long time as a receptacle for the holy water in the church of St. Michael on the Heiligenberg, where it was found.

In the preceding century all these antiquities were removed to Mannheim, and placed amongst the collection of antiquities there, where they are now still to be seen. Still in the beginning of this century, the ceremony of the consecration of the castle church was celebrated annually on the 1st of May at the castle, booths were erected in the castle yard, and parents bought toys and such like articles for their children, or friends and relations exchanged presents with each other in return.

P.

THE ENGLISH OR THE ELISABETH-BUILDING.

The foundations of this building belong to the grand fortifications of the castle which Louis V. had constructed, therefore we request our reader to refer to them in the wanderings through the same; we will only confine ourselves here to the account of the foundation and destruction of the Elisabeth-building; so let us return to the historical facts of our wandering. FREDERICK IV. died in the flower of his age in 1610, and was succeeded to the Electoral throne by his son FREDERICK V. a youth, who had scarcely attained his fifteenth year, and was placed under the guardianship of his cousin the Palsgrave John II. of Deux-ponts. In 1613 this Elector married ELISABETH the only daughter of JAMES STUART (James I. of England), and grand-daughter of the unfortunate MARY STUART.

Soon afterwards this young prince caused the building of this stately palace to be commenced on the northern wall of LOUIS V., the noble style of which we have still an opportunity of witnessing in its ruins. — When FREDERICK V. returned from London, where he had been to celebrate his nuptials, he ordered the architect of his court JEAN SOLOMON DE CAUS, a Norman and experienced man in his art, to erect the great water-works and gardens, of which we now only see a few of the sad remains and which we shall describe more fully in our third wandering through the castle-gardens. The english building was united to the big tower (P. 1) the lower foundations of which together with most of the fortifications were erected by LOUIS V.

This big tower was 235 feet high, 90 feet in diameter and its walls 20 feet thick; in the interior it had seven stories, communicating with each other by a little turret adjoining, enclosing a winding staircase. FREDERICK V. caused the roof to be taken off, without shaking it, by the architect PETER CARL of Nüremberg, the former walls to be pulled down to the plinth, and a spacious lighted hall (P. 2) that could contain 100 tables to be erected and to communicate with the english building.

Towards the Elisabeth-garden, the wanderer will

perceive two beautiful statues in sandstone, the one representing Louis V., and the other Frederick V., between them, on a stone tablet is the following inscription:

LUDOVICUS COM. PAL. R. ELEC. DUX BAVAR. MOLEM HANC EXSTRUXIT A. MDXXXIII. FRIDERICUS V COM. PAL. R. ELEC. S. R. I. VICARIUS BAVAR. DUX AD ZONAM USQ. DESTRUXIT, REFECIT FORNICIBUS DISTINXIT, COENACULI ALTITUDINI XXXIII. PED. ADDIDIT, COLUMNAM TOTIUS TECTI MOLEM SUSTINENTEM E MEDIO SUSTULIT IMMOTO INCORRUPTOQUE TECTO, HANC MONUMENTA POSUIT. A. S. MDCXIX. [1])

Frederick endowed with brilliant qualities, might have become the happiest sovereign of his people, for he ruled over a state blessed by nature in a manner inferior to few other lands, nay even resembling the garden of Eden; but by an insatiable ambition he brought unutterable ruin upon the country he was destined to govern; instigated by his wife, he listened to the dangerous appeal, and accepted the royal crown of Bohemia; left for that country, and in 1620 lost his crown at the battle of the White Mountain, near Prague, against the Emperor Ferdinand.

This election to the crown of Bohemia, which took place on the 16th August 1619 in Prague, and which fell upon Frederick V. gained for him, all the rest of his life, nothing but a crown of thorns.

On the 25th September of the same year he left the

---

[1]) Louis, Count Palatine of the Rhine and Elector, Duke of Bavaria, had this immense work built in the year 1533 — Frederick V., Count Palatine of the Rhine, Elector, and Vicar of the Holy Roman Empire, Duke of Bavaria, caused it to be raised to the entablature, reconstructed and ornamented with a vaulted ceiling, added 33 feet to the height of the dining room, and the pillars which bore the whole weight of the roof to be taken away from the centre, without shaking the roof, in the year of Grace 1619."

beautiful Palatinate to meet with unbounded misery and only to return to it as a fugitive without crown or lands; as for Heidelberg and the castle of his ancestors, he never saw them again. His departure was preceded by a variety of religious ceremonies; but the people seemed to be seized with fearful forebodings, for every where was to be observed on the countenances of these inhabitants of the Palatinate, in other respects always smiling, the expression of sorrow and care. The mother of the newly-elected King of Bohemia, the accomplished LOUISA JULIANA of NASSAU-ORANGE, looked after him for a long time from the windows of the castle on his departure, with maternal anxiety, and overcome with a dreadful presentiment, her eyes full of tears and in a sorrowful voice, exclaimed: „Alas! the Palatinate is now going to Bohemia!!!"

Frederick, as before observed, never more returned to the seat of his ancestors as his mother but too truly presaged, for the magnificent castle and the whole country suffered most terribly from the fury of the fiercest wars. He died of grief at Mentz in 1632.

Frederick V. is one of the ancestors on the mother's side of the present reigning house of Great Britain.

What traveller is not moved with admiration at the gigantic construction of the big tower, when he looks down from the high windows of the english building into the terrible depth below or when he finds himself at the foot of the tower, and casts his eyes up to its height, which only now exists in a small part.

The Count Palatine and Elector CHARLES LOUIS, son of the unfortunate FREDERICK V., or as he was nick-named at that time a „king of one winter", assembled together those of his subjects who were dispersed about in all countries, by the frightful calamities of the war, and endeavoured by a wise administration of his state, to heal up the wounds of his unfortunate country, that had been so deeply oppressed, and to restore the much damaged castle of his forefathers, which, in the description of the different buildings, we have had the opportunity of delineating.

He married his daughter ELISABETH CHARLOTTE to Duke PHILIP of ORLEANS, brother of LOUIS XIV.; this was the occasion of the breaking out of the war of the Orleans' succession, his only son CHARLES dying without issue, and which war through the furious troops of Melac, plunged this beautiful land into so much distress. The noble character of this worthy prince is still preserved to posterity by the following trait.

Already during the time of the thirty years' war, the castle, as we have related, had been often destroyed, but restored as much as possible by CHARLES LOUIS, who reigned from 1650 to 1680; but the real paternal care for his people, with which this noble prince was penetrated, will show itself in the following letter he wrote in 1673, to MARSHAL TURENNE who then had his head quarters at Schwetzingen, and who afterwards was killed near Sasbach by a cannon ball from the enemy.

He wrote to the french General who was the predecessor of Count Melac, and who had laid waste the Palatinate aboute fifteen years previous to the latter, as follows:

„What you are now practising upon my land, cannot possibly proceed from the orders of his Most Christian Majesty [1]); I cannot consider it otherwise than a personal spite you have against me; but it is unjust that my poor subjects should suffer for what you perhaps may have at heart against me, therefore I beg you to appoint the time, place and weapons, that we may end our quarrel."

---

[1]) A title given to the Kings of France by the Pope.

But the french Marshal did not however expose his life against that of the chivalrous German Palsgrave; but from that time he spared the Palatinate more, and left Schwetzingen.

CHARLES LOUIS died at Edingen, a village between Heidelberg and Mannheim, in a peasant's orchard 1680, and his son CHARLES, who but little resembled his father, succeeded him in the Electoral dignity.

The large hall in the big tower was then transformed into a theatre, where the prince himself acted. He also built Fort Charles with the Charles Tower, of the latter not a single trace is remaining. The Elector Charles when in England received his degree as Doctor, and likewise the Order of the Garter, consequently he caused the insignia of this order and the motto to be carved in his arms, which are to be seen in stone on the fort Charles. He died in 1685, when the war of the Orleans' succession broke out, which proved so fatal for the Palatinate.

The wanderer has already gone through with me the principal buildings of this ALHAMBRA of Germany, and having endeavoured to describe to him its several destinies, I will now proceed with the second wandering through the fortifications of our magnificent castle.

IV.

WANDERINGS

THROUGH THE FORTIFICATIONS OF THE RUINS OF THE CASTLE OF HEIDELBERG.

———

This wandering is of special interest to the lover of the art of war, and without being arranged in chronological order, we will only treat of it as a tour through the fortifications, the principal buildings of which have been already described in the preceding accounts.

The most interesting points are marked with small letters beginning with *a* etc.

When the wanderer ascends the hill on which the buildings of this princely castle are raised, and has left the houses of the City of the Muses from the side of the Corn Market, he will reach the exterior footpath of the castle or the Chancery[1] path (*a*), which is bordered on the right by a wall of support (Stützmauer)

———

[1] Another road to the castle, joins the castle or upper town with the lower part, the foot of the Burgweg beginning at the right and leading up steps to the exterior gate of the castle, this is called the „kurze Buckel“ (or short-cut). On going up this path, towards the middle, you will see to the left a house (vide the Situation Plan D. S.) in which there lives a very aged, but still a hale and hearty man, called Daniel Schlagenauf, one of those originals that are seldom to be met with, a sort of living chronicle, but like many other old chroniclers, are not always very correct in recording facts; this man however has employed the whole of a long life, and made many sacrifices in collecting a large quantity of antiques, well worthy of inspection.

and from the inscriptions on the tablets that are seen on it, it has been constructed and renewed by several Electors, such as:

1. Tablet: Count Palatine Frederick, Elector, built me 1552 (Frederick II.).
2. „ Count Palatine Charles Louis, Elector, built me 1651.
3. „ Count Palatine Charles Theodore, Elector, repaired me 1751.
4. „ Elector Charles Frederick of Baden rebuilt me 1805.

To the left the road is planted with trees. Not far from the above mentioned tablets it divides and leads to the right towards Fort Charles, while to the left it conducts to the shady walks of the garden.

The Fort Charles (*b*) formerly strongly fortified is raised upon three terraces, that is, the two first being front-courts and the third the real fort. In the second higher front-court, the walled up entrance to the interior, is still to be seen, above which are the electoral arms (*c*) cut out in stone, and bearing the insignia of the Order of the Garter in very ordinary work; but the motto of the order: „Honi soit qui mal y pense" is easily to be read. Both these front-courts were strongly armed with different pieces of artillery to judge from the embrasures. But as the entrance to the interior of the fort is walled up, in order to get to it, I must conduct the wanderer by another path up a little staircase, which like the others in this road has been built in modern times — for it is certain cannons could not have been carried up such steep steps — where to the left he will see a little door blocked up (*d*), not far from which he will pass through a larger gate (*e*) a little higher up, into the interior of the fort. From here to the right towards the east are seen fragments of walls where the Charles Tower (*f*) was joined to this fortification, and which the Elector who gave his name to it had built at the same time as the fort in 1683; this date may be perceived by the wanderer on the arms above mentioned. Formerly on the place of the Charles Fort there stood a large Tennis-court, surrounded with a gallery, the Elector had this pulled down and transformed it into a fort.

Several vaults are still to be seen, one of them conducted to a door at the foot of the octagon tower, but this door is also walled up; it was called afterwards the fox's hole (g). From there a corridor appropriated to the sentinels led further; many of these corridors in fort Charles are furnished with stone sentry-boxes.

Now, wanderer, follow me through the gate where we entered this fort, — demolished in the time of the war of the Orleans' succession — into the little hall (h) and from thence into the interior road of the castle, where you will see to your left the old colossal foundation-walls of the former arsenal (i), which appear to owe their origin to a more remote period. — FREDERICK the Victorious had those already constructed in 1455 on the remains of the older walls. It is plainly to be seen where the French had trenched to lay their train, in order to spring up these colossal walls. But the mine did not perfectly succeed, for the old walls resisted the force of the gunpowder; here are likewise to be seen the places where the attempts at mining were afterwards repaired. Opposite to the arsenal there is a road to the right which on ascending will bring you to a door leading into the little Battery (k), an important fortification, stretching itself almost the whole length of the north side the castle towards the Neckar, and is raised in three compartments in the form of terraces towards the east. [1])

----

[1]) At the foot of the high wall of this battery, where several

Close adjoining to this battery is the large Hall (*l*), which Frederick IV. had built, together with the large beautiful balcony 1601—1607 upon the old castle walls (*m*).

The large hall consists of crossed vaults in which may still be seen on one of the key-stones, the arms of the Palatinate with the imperial orb. These crossed vaults repose on doric wall-pillars, and the light falls from the north into the hall; at the east end there is an ante-room used for the guard, and at the west end two similar ones.

From the inner road of the castle the wanderer will come to a gate, which was formerly entered by means of a draw-bridge into the large hall, from where you arrived at the battery through a door and up a staircase. Under this large hall there are also vaults, which served as guard-rooms, and three other halls (*n*) used to keep the cannon. Out of one of the first of these vaults in the back ground, is still to be seen the old castle, as it was built by Louis V. on granite rocks. A sewer partly filled up with dirt, leads to the Frederick's building in one of these vaults. I had this place that was formerly covered over with wild brambles and briars, transformed into a pleasant garden, from whence you may enjoy a most delightful view over the town, the Neckar and the valley of the Rhine. When you pass to the little battery round the corner building of the balcony — now called the garden of the balcony — you will see a place where the Swedish colonel-in-chief FULKO HUNKS — an Englishman by birth who com-

---

breaches have been made, a ditch now almost filled up, runs along the battery, in this ditch is still to be seen the upper part of an arched doorway, through which I went, and came to a vault which formerly led into the dungeons of the lower battery, but now for the most part full of rubbish.

manded in the castle under Abel Moda — deposited the heart of his companion-in-arms and serjeant-major Abraham Meppel.

A large stone (o) with a latin inscription marks the spot, and translated into English runs thus:

> „To his blessed memory. Stop, O wanderer!
> Fulko Hunks, a Briton, beseeches you to mark the spot where the true and manly heart of his Achates and serjeant-major is deposited. He died fighting victoriously on the third day of June 1635. Envy his valour and depart.“

A latin anagram follows this epitaph, but it is difficult to be made out, in English this is about the meaning:

> „As a brave man, I fought badly,
> In Meerhausen I retrieved my fame.
> Fulko Hunks, colonel-in-chief of the troops at war, has placed this stone in sincere devotion.“

This battery or garden of the balcony was at the end of the last century and the beginning of the present, left at the disposition of the commandants of the place (the last was M. von Kügel) who, with the artillery ground (grand battery) generally made use of it as a farm.

. Under the battery you may see the many attempts to blow it up or to enter it by breaches. Next to the building which contains the great tun, begins the great foundation of the Elisabeth or English Building (p) which Louis V. built in 1533, together with the big tower.

Here also the wanderer will observe the raging destruction which the flames of war have spread amongst these superb buildings; for two enormous deep breaches, or attempts at springing by mine, have considerably tended to help the hand of time to destroy by degrees that work of Louis, which seemed as if it were to last to eternity. — A small door leads from the west end

74

of the little battery to these foundations, and to the few remains of the once far celebrated BIG TOWER (q) where you may plainly see the different gradations of the six stories.

Two dark openings, which the wanderer can see over the centre in the interior of the big tower, and which I have climbed up, lead to what were formerly secret apartments; but close to the ground, you may see a gate-way (r) half filled up, through which you may enter and penetrate for a long way till you are under the so-called rotunda of the artillery-ground or the great rampart built by Louis, where the way then divides, and is filled up with rubbish.

On casting a glance over the gigantic wall on the west side of this rampart, we perceive its half round tower, called the ROTUNDA (s) half destroyed, and in which from the Elisabeth garden you may still see a little door from where you can ascend to the top, by means of a winding staircase and penetrate far into the secret corridors which are said to have intertwined each other under this peaceful garden shaded with lime-trees. The entrance to this winding staircase is still visible from the artillery-ground, but filled up with large quarry stones. This stone winding staircase of 10 feet in diameter was quite filled up with rubbish, but I had it entirely cleared out, and one can now descend 126 steps, where three openings lead to the three different divisions of the tower; at the end of the staircase there is a fourth opening closed in with an iron door, to which an ancient German padlock is attached. This lower doorway leads through an arched vaulted passage to the lowest parts of the big tower, 191 feet distant.

FREDERICK V. had the former cupola of this rotunda taken off, and surrounded it with a balustrade, which was destroyed in the Orleans' war.

According to the saying of some of the old folks of

Heidelberg who pretend to have heard it again from other old people, they maintain that from this big tower, a secret passage led into the town, which we only look upon as tradition; but let us return to a gothic gateway or postern-gate (*t*) in the lower foundations of the Elisabeth-building, and which is half filled up; through this we reach a broad massive staircase with 50 steps, up which the cannon may probably have been dragged or let down. This staircase which leads from the cellar under the Rupertina-chapel to the lower part of the big tower, seems to have served to transport ammunition and pieces of ordnance by means of this way into the fortifications of this part of the castle. But we will not pursue this route any further; for having mounted this staircase let us repair to the right to another massive staircase (*u*) which, as well as the entrance and the doorway that leads from there to the old castle wall, I have had entirely cleared of the rubbish, and through a new upper staircase have made it accessible (*v*). It is interesting to see the attempts the French made here to blow up the strong building of Louis V. and the graceful palace of Frederick V.; for what did not succeed then, would evidently have occurred, if two strong pillars had not been placed afterwards under the large crevice caused by the springing of the mine.

But having arrived at the fortifications of the remoter times, for example behind the chapel of Rupert I, and Rudolph's paltry commencement of the building of the castle, we turn round again, ascend another staircase and arrive at the covered battery of Louis V., a gallery (*w*), in which were two cannons; the walls are 24 feet thick and faced from the exterior with large hewn stones; this battery served as a cover to the castle ditch towards the south. Opposite to this covered battery we reach the north side of the lower foundations of the Elisabeth-building, where formidable loop-holes are likewise to be seen; these two batteries formed the understructure of the English building.

On going a little further to the west, you pass a little gate-way, formerly furnished with a port-cullis that is easily to be seen in the masonry work; from here you mount another staircase and arrive at newer fortifications which date from the Elector FREDERICK V. and his grand-son Elector CHARLES. An outlet formerly provided with ditches and drawbridges led from here to the grand rampart of LOUIS V. (y), which was called the „Great Battery“, and which to-day is known by the name of the Elisabeth or Artillery-ground; it received the latter name from this place having been granted in 1700 to the corps of the civil artillery company for their use and place of drill; therefore a little building was erected before the big tower for the keeping of their cannon, but was pulled down when this exercising ground was transferred to another spot in 1805. Before leaving the artillery-ground, you may observe behind the big tower a wall with loop-holes (z), which at that time was used as a garrison for the great battery; but we will pursue the path to the old wall behind the Rupertina-chapel, and look round a little upon this interesting spot; then descend and wander through the crevices made by the springing of the mines in the castle ditch (aa) and which then could be filled with from 6 to 7 feet of water; here the wanderer will behold the old grey lower foundations of the Rupertina-chapel, the Rudolph's and Rupert's building to the Louis' tower (bb), called later in the XVII. century „Never-empty“ (Nimmerleer), and to the right the high rampart of Louis, which discovers at its southern extremity a gate (cc), through which he can wander from about 40 to 50 paces to the south-west, afterwards the way is stopped up with rubbish. At a certain height you very plainly see a narrow way (dd) along the rampart, from where the sluices were let up and down. The little passage in the Louis' building served the same purpose, from which, where now the crevice is that was caused by the springing of the mine, a door led into the interior of the tower. When you now turn round the corner of the large castle ditch, you will see to the right, from the false economy of a former architect, the wall deprived of its beautiful quarry stones, and which are now carried to Schwetzingen. To the left are the ruins of the old fortifications, and near the big watch-tower is an old ruined staircase (*ee*) that led to a door, from where the prisoners were let down into the deep dungeon of the watch-tower. A clear trout-stream now runs through this ditch, and supplies several fountains of the town with water.

The bridge (*ff*) and the high watch-tower were erected by Louis V. in 1541 upon the deep castle ditch. The formidable square watch-tower (*gg*) is 43 feet broad on each side, built entirely with hewn stones and rises to a very considerable height. In the cross-arches of the gate you can see the arms of the Electors on the key-stones. The two badly constructed figures of the knights, and which offend the eye of the artist, as well as the lions, were first placed by Frederick II. on the watch-tower, and the centre coat of arms, that is now wanting, is said to have been beautifully wrought in silver.

The tower and bridge must have appeared more interesting at the beginning of this century, when that part looking towards the watch-tower was furnished with a draw-bridge; but even here the bad taste of an unskilful architect caused a detrimental effect; he had the beautiful square-stones between the watch-tower and the blown-up tower taken away, raised the bridge with paltry arches and closed it up to the entrance, while the wall deprived of its ornament, is now falling with rapid steps into decay.

Let us now wander under the arches of the bridge, where you will observe under the last one, a hole filled with spring-water, in which trout are preserved; then wander to the left towards the east side of the watch-tower, where you may descend by an opening made through the thick wall into the frightful dungeon of the tower (*hh*) which I have had completely cleared out and rendered accessible. The unfortunate creatures who were thrown into this dungeon, were let down through a door next to the winding staircase, and from there by a windlass were precipitated to the bottom. Directly before you is to be seen a covered outwork (*ii*), now in ruins, built by the Elector CHARLES, but here nature seems to have striven to contribute her share to the embellishment of the scene; for exactly on this spot an immense lime-tree (*kk*) has sprung up, dividing itself into two parts, from the bottom up to the most elevated branches, and which by a singular freak of nature is very broad from the base to the top and thereby likewise unproportionably thin, that is to say, one of the trunks is 4 feet in breadth with only a thickness of 8 to 9 inches; the other 3 feet in breadth, and only from 6 to 7 inches thick, a proportion which is carried on throughout its branches.

Through the ruins of this outwork a gate [1]) leads to the trout preserves, near which several steps conduct to the source of the lower PRINCES' FOUNTAIN (*ll*) furnished with two pipes, and is celebrated for the abundancy of its pure water.

This part of the castle-ditch to the north outlet near the great covered outwork (caponnière), is now called the VALLEY OF MATTHISSON, because it was here that Matthisson, the immortal poet of nature, used to walk, and where he wrote his beautiful poem „HEIDELBERG CASTLE" while he was living here, in his capacity of tutor to a Livonian Count in 1787.

---

[1]) From here the wanderer can proceed further without a guide.

To the right you will see a small house (*mm*) enclosing a pretty little spring, surrounded with stones and shells; it was erected by CHARLES THEODORE, and easily to be recognised by the latin inscription on it:

> „New and extremely healthy spring intended by CHARLES THEODORE, the father of the country, and ELISABETH AUGUSTA, the mother of the country, to serve as a new source to health."

The interior of this building, the river god and the other objects, are the remains of an ancient grotto found formerly in the large plantations with their grottoes and vaults, and which we shall treat of further in a wandering through the gardens. In the interior there is also a latin inscription to be seen, which means in English:

> „Healthy by nature; clear through Bayer's care."

CHARLES THEODORE had water brought from this spring to Mannheim every day. — Opposite to this small house, you may perceive one of the most picturesque ruins of the castle, the so-called blown-up tower (*nn*), 82 feet in diameter, with strong walls 20 feet thick.

The wanderer will stand amazed at the sight of this wondrous ruin, which formerly served to contain the powder-magazine built by FREDERICK I. the Victorious, but blown up by order of a French general in 1693. However its walls resisted the force of the powder, for the part blown up remains undemolished and towers like a rock from out of its grave, which for many centuries to come will serve as an accusing monument of the devastations committed by Melac.

From a report of this general to Louis XIV. three French pioneers were missing when this mine was sprung, and more than a century after, a vault was accidentally opened in the proximity of the tower, and three squeletons, probably the remains of these unfortunate pioneers were found, who thought themselves secure in this spot when the explosion took place, and which prepared for them this dreadful end.

Opposite to the blown-up tower, the wanderer will perceive a ridge of granite rocks, which, if he be skilled in geology, will prove interesting to him; for it is a remarkable fact that the granite rising from the depth is covered with mighty coats of a conglomerated substance, principally of a granite gravel composed of fragments of granite and rubble, to be distinguished from the original granite by the mass of several new granite streaks which have formed themselves up to the ruins of the rock.

We will now proceed by a passage dug through the DOUBLE-VAULT (*oo*), the lower part of which formerly served as a fortification for the defence of the little ditch, and the upper as conduit. If we turn to the right through this passage, in the corridor for a few steps further, we shall find it, walled up; but formerly this upper part of the vault conducted the water of the Friesenberg to the large grotto and the different waterworks, and then under the blown-up tower to the grand fountain of the castle-yard. But when we go along this passage to the left, we shall follow the conduit a little further, when the lower part then divides itself, while the passage to the left under the conduit guides to a cross-vault, partly in ruins, under the blown-up tower, and that to the right to the large casemate (*pp*).

This casemate is entirely preserved; I have had it completely cleared of the rubbish with which it was nearly filled to the top, and there is now a commodious passage through it. Underneath there is a lateral drain (*qq*), visible in the centre of the passage, leading to the Neckar, which may have been the cause of the saying that there was a subterranean passage from the castle under the Neckar.

At the northern extremity of the long casemate a

staircase leads down to the great Caponière (*rr*) which protected the entrance to the ditch, and the eastern back part of the castle, covered the Friesenberg, arranged for 8 guns and 15 falconets erected by the Elector Charles in 1683. This beautiful vault is now the only spiral one belonging to the whole castle; I cleared the whole of the staircase and the vault of its rubbish, and rendered the interior accessible to every one without danger.

From here you ascend the long casemate again, which was formerly in communication with the lowest part of the Library tower, and also by a row of partitioned casemates with Fort Charles.

These partitioned casemates consisted in two rows, one upon another; while the one led to the little battery and the other to Fort Charles.

Having ascended from the long casemate you may see an outwork (*ss*) which served to flank the entrance, and was furnished with large and small pieces of artillery, and from there we arrive at the old wall of the castle, now transformed into a delightful walk along the eastern buildings.

Now we arrive at a staircase, which we descend, and by a door way reach the remains of the above mentioned casemate (*tt*), where the wanderer enters the third compartment of the little battery raised in terraces, mentioned at the beginning of this description, and with which we will now terminate our wandering through the fortifications.

You have now with me, respected wanderer, finished this tour amongst the ruins, and have seen many interesting spots, that I have endeavoured to preserve for posterity; but numerous vaults, perhaps of the most interesting construction, various passages in the bowels of the earth crossing each other like a labyrinth under the castle, are probably still covered up with dust and may, if circumstances permit, be cleared out and rendered accessible.

Let us now cast a general look upon the fortifications we have just frequented, and consider that at the commencement of their construction the terrible force and power of gunpowder was not known, and when afterwards used in the contentions and battles of the thirty-years' war, when Vauban's system of fortifications did not exist, our Castle of Heidelberg defended by formidable towers, gigantic ramparts, fire-proof casemates and strong batteries, was no unimportant place in the history of the wars of that period.

The powerful hand of time however which metamorphoses every thing in life, has taught us to construct more solid works; but the creations of our forefathers, by which we have brought things to perfection, will nevertheless still remain most interesting to us.

———

WANDERINGS

THROUGH THE GARDENS OF THE RUINS OF HEIDELBERG CASTLE.

————

The castle gardens of Heidelberg have such charms as art cannot reproduce; for what at last is human power compared with eternal and creative nature, but really little less than a mole hill to the gigantic mountains of the Alps!

The most beautiful of one of the most charming spots in Germany, is the garden of the castle of Heidelberg, from whence the eye is delighted with verdant fields, dark forests, rivers, mountains and valleys, and enjoys a most varied change in its surrounding towns and villages; here the regenerative hand of art and labour must not sway, but simply lend its aid in case of necessity to render this spot still more agreeable to the eye of man.

Here are roads to be made level, there groups of trees to be arranged according to their varied shades of green, or to thin the forests, in order to lay open to the sight delightful prospects both far and near, or plant groves and bushes, the haunts of lovely singing birds; but above all carefully to nurse and tend those venerable trees which stand in such perfect harmony with the ruin, and to undertake nothing that could in any way modernise it.

This is in the face of such charms which the environs offer to us, the task of art, and I have proposed to myself to undertake that task, and as far as it lies in my power, to see this important resolution carried out.

The superintendant of the forests Gatterer has the merit of having had the first idea of regenerating this garden, formerly so magnificent, and later entirely ruined, giving it as it were a new shape and of making it accessible to the inhabitants and strangers; for since the disastrous year of 1764, — where the lightning, as we have related, struck the New-court and almost burnt the whole castle down — till 1803 the garden was let and used for the cultivation of fruit and vegetables.

Mr. de Leonhard relates in his excellent Guide-book a report of Gatterer's on the farming of the castle-gardens at that time: „the principal part of the garden with the dwelling of the Castellain in the castle-yard was let out on the 31ˢᵗ of July 1798 for 12 years to the state pensioner and private secretary LEGER at a yearly rent of 400 florins.

He cultivated corn and vegetables, and added to it a little farm, but could not succeed on account of the bad soil and want of manure; he determined therefore to lay it out in a small plantation of succory-roots (in the spring of 1803) and established a manufactory of succory - coffee. LEGER petitioned the college of the counsellors Aulic at Mannheim for support, and obtained a deduction of 150 florins in his lease fore thre years.

His predecessor in the farm WEHRLE paid 200 florins per annum — afterwards only fl. 150 — and even then was reduced in the strictest sense of the word to a state of beggary." At that time fl. 150 and now? — *Tempora mutantur!*

In 1804 the reform commenced, and since then the gardens have been partly used by the University as a forest botanical garden.

The Director of the garden at that time, ZEYHER

projected the plan which is still preserved in the castle. Our garden has only been extended like the castle itself successively, having been very much limited in the commencement. However LOUIS III. bought the landed property adjoining in 1434, and under FREDERICK V. when it was entirely new laid out, it arrived at its greatest extent, and considerably exceeded its present limits; but let us recommence our wandering where from the exterior Castle-way the roads divide, and instead of going to the right to Fort Charles, direct our path to the left round the angle on the right of the fort, where the Charles Tower formerly stood, no trace of which is remaining, and wander up a slight ascent under a roof of foliage — the so-called alley of accacias — to the south, till we arrive at the outwork built by the Elector CHARLES, and leaving to the right the homely valley of Matthisson — formerly the Castle-ditch — turning to the Friesenberg, then to the left, we have the little valley reclining towards the town and separates the Friesenberg from the Jetta-hill which formerly was larger, for the path in which we are, as well as the garden land on the right, is only raised ground. FREDERICK V. the unfortunate King of Bohemia on his return from London in 1613 where he had celebrated his nuptials with the english Princess Elisabeth, gave orders to the architect of his court John Solomon de Caus to construct a royal pleasure garden on the Friesenberg [1]) and the Jetta-hill. Formerly the Electoral park stood between the Friesenberg and the Jetta-hill. Rocks were blown up and levelled, hollows filled up, and then Master CAUS commenced his work, which he likewise finished in a few years, and erected on this rough declivity of the hill a most magnificent garden which at that time

---

[1]) The Friesenberg, according to old historians, is said to have received its name from the roughness of its ground.

was not to be equalled. Three sides of the castle were surrounded by these plantations.

Caverns, grottoes, waterworks, statues of all kinds, terraces of flowers, groves, orangeries, trees and exotic plants varied the scene, and continually presented to the astonished eye a new object of admiration, till in 1619, when the fatal Bohemian war broke out and not only put a stop to the work which was almost finished, but even prepared for the most part of these new creations a premature ruin.

But observe, wanderer, the colossal lining of the wall of the Friesenberg, and admire with me the art with which the clever architect seemed to have constructed it for times immemorial. Solomon de Caus writes among other things on the subject of this garden in his work: „*Hortus Palatinus a Friderico rege Bohemiæ Electore Palatino Heidelbergæ extructus Salomone de Caus, Francofr. 1620*“:

„In the year 1616 the Elector Palatine rendered his castle celebrated by a garden truly royal, and magnificently ornamented it with exotic plants, most artistically arranged, principally with fountains and waterworks and some so arranged as to perform music. — In this garden is to be seen amongst others an orangery, in which are thirty large orange-trees, each about 25 feet high and 400 trees of smaller growth; in 1619 the large ones were sixty years old when they were taken in their full height with their roots and earth, placed into cases of a particular form expressly constructed for them, and transported from the old seigneurial garden in the suburb up to the top of the mountain into this new garden with considerable trouble and labour. Every year an orangery was constructed for them about Michaelmas 180 feet long and 32 feet broad; it was a wooden building heated throughout the winter with four stoves.

The flower-garden was 80 feet long and 200 feet in

breadth, with a little pond in which all the waters from the garden concentrated.

The different trees had likewise various waterworks constructed about them, which took a whole hour to put them into play.

The greatest part of this work, with the exception of the musical arrangement was entirely completed, and terminated with a large grotto, a fish pond and several smaller grottoes."

Such was the description of our worthy Solomon de Caus [1]).

Let us now, my dear wanderer, ascend the steps, and you will still see the same yew trees and the old yoke-elms of that period; follow me further to the end of the terrace, and enjoy the delightful prospect over the Neckar and the surrounding mountains, the castle ruins, the extensive and fertile plain of the Rhine and the distant mountains of the Haardt wich bound the horizon, and at this sight you will surely not regret the waterworks and fantastic grottoes of Master Caus. This terrace is supported by the immense lined wall (1), which, for greater solidity, arched niches with buttresses have been artistically constructed, behind which the depth has been filled up with stones and rubbish. —

At the northern extremity of the terrace there arose formerly out of the depths of the little wood of the Carmelites a building in the form of a tower, which with the exception of a few insignificant remains has disappeared in the course of time. Under the first and

---

[1]) Solomon de Caus is said to have gone to France after the breaking out of the thirty-years' war, and already at that period fore-told the mighty power of steam, and drew up the plan of a steam-engine; but the fruits of his meditations were looked upon as the effu-sions of a disordered brain, and this great man treated as a madman by his contemporaries, died in poverty in a hospital of a brokenheart.

smallest of the arches a subterranean passage led to the granite rock upwards of 90 feet high, and must formerly have served for carrying down the building materials or for draining off the superfluous water.

A path at the foot of the terrace leads to the little wood of the Carmelites, belonging to the Castle-gardens, and a second at the other extremity also leading into the wood; these two paths join each other in the little wood, and conduct you to the upper part of the town. The octagon (2) you see here between a chesnut plantation, is in bad taste and was constructed in 1771, to serve as a shelter for persons overtaken by the rain.

From here you will direct your path to the south, where on passing before a little pond you will arrive at the large grotto (3), the entrance to which is artistically formed and ornamented on the top with two obelisks and all sorts of figures of animals. The interior of the grotto was divided into two compartments and decorated with stones of various colours, coral and shells. In the back ground the stream of a fountain passed through a gold ball and the water flowed down the rock. Before the grotto opposite to the aforementioned entrance, was to be seen lying upon rocks in the middle of a pond the colossal statue of the Rhine (4), which for many years, although in ruins, has mounted guard before the cave.

This old figure of the Rhine god though terribly mutilated, I have had restored as much as possible, and placed upon a bed of rocks in the pond, which was choked up with mud, and which I had completely cleaned out, thinking thereby to embellish the situation by its picturesque appearance, and likewise to preserve the statue from total ruin.

From here there are several terraces that contained extensive vaulted spaces of different dimensions with shell-work, coral and party-coloured stones; these vaults served partly as reservoirs for fish, conservatories for trees in the winter, and for baths. The two columns (*6*) which you observe a little further to the south on the first terrace formerly ornamented a semi-circular walled niche, now in decay and replaced by a lined wall. In this vault was the fountain of Neptune. The water-god was reposing with his trident on the head of a dolphin. On the upper part of the niche there was a latin inscription in stone, indicating the foundation of the garden and which signified in English:

„Frederick, King of Bohemia, Palsgrave of the Rhine and Elector has consecrated this spot formerly dedicated to the gods of the forests and the chase — to the god of the gardens, by levelling the tops of the mountains, filling up the valleys and ornamenting them with aqueducts, fountains, statues, plants, flowers and immense high trees transplanted by a most particular art from the garden of the suburb, and completed the work in the year of grace 1619."

On the top of all this towered the statue of Frederick V. in cloak and armour 15 feet high.

From this spot towards the west runs a long wall (*7*) in which were several grottoes and vaults, some have fallen to pieces, and one of them is still used as a reservoir for trout (*8*). Into one of these last vaults (*9*) partly in decay, but still showing a considerable space, you enter by an opening at the top entirely concealed by ivy and bushes. Here near to this opening a detachment of Prussian soldiers had posted themselves during the disastrous revolution of 1849, when in pursuit of a party of insurgents, and not many steps removed from them, was the entrance to this aforesaid vault, covered with brambles, where a number of the revolutionists had concealed themselves for several days; they could overhear almost every word of their pursuers, and when the latter had retired, escaped further.

Now let us turn to the House of Refreshment or Tavern (*10*) which is surrounded on the east and south by high

trees, and where the wanderer may regale himself with excellent meats and drinks, and on several days of the week
his ear be delighted with choice musical productions.

The celebrated and spirited author TIECK does not
seem to have been delighted with the innovations he
met with in the castle gardens, from what he said on
the spot in his time:

„The true feeling for nature is wanting in our time
as much as she is always looking for it; for not only
regular gardens are converted into romantic ones, which
shocks the taste of our times, but even wild places really
romantic are persecuted and forced into the rule and
construction of modern horticulture. Around the large
and admirable ruins of Heidelberg, there reigned such
a green, fresh, poetical and wild solitude, which harmo-
nised so beautifully with the decayed towers, the vast
courts and the divine nature; all this produced upon the
soul the effect of a finished poem of the middle age. I
was so enchanted with this single spot upon our German land, that its fresh and verdant image hovered for
years over the dreams of my imagination; but some time
ago, I also found here a sort of park, which it is true
offers to the wanderer many a charming spot and many
a beautiful prospect and where commodious paths lead
to places that could formerly only be climbed with danger, and where one can obtain refreshments safely and
securely in agreeable apartments; however all these advantages are not equivalent to the grand and only beauty,
which has been here destroyed with the best intention.“

The intellectual poet was certainly in the right if the
hand of art predominated in our plantations; but, as I
said at the commencement of this section, it should only
assist nature, for it would only serve to disfigure this
imposing picture, that dame nature has created in union
with the destructive hand of time. We do not think we
exagerate, in supposing that nine out of ten of the pil-

grims who visit the ruins of the castle, would rather prefer approaching them by clean and easy paths, than according to Tieck's wish to expose themselves to danger, to sink up to their knees in mud, or to break their necks by climbing up steep cliffs in a romantic manner, exhausted by hunger and thirst.

Behind the tavern against the line of wall, the wanderer will see an interesting tree, that has survived the storms of the thirty-years' war and that of the Orleans' succession; it is a *Thuja occidentalis* (*11*) or North American cypress, planted on this spot in 1618, but now a decrepid old tree, long since tired of life, and would infallibly have already returned to the bosom of its mother earth, if it had not been fastened with chains to younger trees and esteemed as a relic. Many of its offsprings however grow round about it, and even upon the fragments of wall, that have fallen from the blown-up tower, its seed having been no doubt carried there by the wind or the birds.

We will now pass to the right along the castle-ditch, with the valley of Matthisson, the blown-up tower and the lower fountain of the princes; while to the left agreeable paths through shady alleys or a broad road leads to the upper fountain of the princes (*12*); to reach the reservoir you must descend 15 steps, from whence this delightful spring issues forth through two tubes.

CHARLES PHILIP collected this spring together in 1738, and built the hall over it. Above the entrance you may still see the initials of Charles Philip interwoven in each other with the date of the year 1738, and on the right of the steps as you descend, you will find a latin inscription, which signifies in English: „This fountain was repaired under the direction of Bibiena, and the waters rendered clearer by the assiduous care of Henry Neb."

The Elector CHARLES PHILIP, who left Heidelberg

the 14th October 1720, and fixed his residence at Mannheim, had, like his successor CHARLES THEODORE, water
brought from here to Mannheim twice every day.

On proceeding further past the Bridge-house to the
left, we perceive several vaults, which may have served
for coach-houses, saddle-rooms, baths &c. (13).

To the right we reach the remains of an arch (14)
and on passing through it come to the great castle rampart; this is the Elisabeth-gate that the youthful Elector
FREDERICK V. built in honour of his beautiful wife in
so short a time, that the construction seems to have
been the work of a magician. For my english readers
who are studying my native language and admire the
beautiful flowers of the garden of German poesy, I now
add a few verses of the poet MAX VON SCHENKENDORF
which refer to this gate:

„Vor Allen, die gesessen
Auf Ruprecht's hohem Thron,
War Einem zugemessen
Der höchste Erdenlohn.
Wie jauchzten rings die Lande
Am Neckar jener Zeit,
Als er vom Engellande
Das Königskind gefreit.
Viel der besten Ritter kamen,
Ihrem Dienste sich zu weih'n.
Dort, wo noch mit ihrem Namen
Prangt ein Thor von rothem Stein,
Liess sie fern die Blicke schweifen
In das weite, grüne Thal,
Nach den Fernen soll sie greifen
In des Herzens falscher Wahl.
Da kam wie Meereswogen,
Wie rother Feuerbrand
Ein bitt'res Weh gezogen
Zum lieben Vaterland.
Die alten Festen bebten,
Es schwand des Glaubens Schein,
Und finst're Mächte strebten,
Die Fremden zogen ein."

The singular sculpture of this arch, where the pillars represent the trunks of trees entwined with ivy, upon which a lizard, a frog, a squirrel and a snail are visible, will for a time occupy our attention.

I have still another remark to make about the ornamental remains of the Elisabethan archway, which forms the entrance to the so-called artillery-ground. During the Easter recess of 1823, a modern Vandal amused himself with destroying and removing the figures of frogs and lizards from these graceful pillars; the introduction of such figures shows that the sculptor was well acquainted with the works of ancient art, for they remind one of those works in Rome, which Metellus caused to be erected by Batrachos and Sauros (frog and lizard) of Sparta; they were wont to ornament their works with the figures of the animals whose names they bore. In the church of St. Lorenzo in Rome, there is still a pillar to be seen, with one of the finest capitals of the ancient times; on one side in the Valuta, a frog is introduced, and on the other a lizard. Undoubtedly this is one of the pillars of Juno, which Metellus had constructed within the portal of his house, by Sauros and Batrachos.

Two female figures, the genii of fortune, hold their cornu-copiae over the arch of the gate, and in the frieze are the imperial globe and two lions, above is the latin inscription: „*Fredericus V. Elisabethae conjugi carissimae A. C. MDCXV.*" — Frederick V. to his dearly beloved wife Elisabeth in the year of Christ 1615.

This entrance adorned on both sides with pillars and architectural ornaments, formerly stood near the aviary, of which only a very small part, a stone covered with ivy, is still to be seen towards the western declivity of the great castle rampart.

The director of the garden, the late Mr. METZGER, relates in his work „Heidelberg Castle", that in the year 1774 this aviary (*15*) under the name of the artillery-

ground, was to be transformed, according to the pro-
position of the director of buildings Mr. de Pigage in
Schwetzingen, into a tavern, to be let out on lease together with the garden; but the enormous expence of
3000 florins for the transformation of this establishment,
was the cause of the plan not being executed. This
aviary, as it was called, together with the Elisabeth-
archway, closed in the whole ·of the artillery-ground.
At the further extremity of the Elisabeth-garden, we
perceive the two statues mentioned before of Louis V.
and FREDERICK V. thickly surrounded with ivy, and a
stone (*16*) which stands here, that was formerly in another place, and relates to us a feat of the Elector Charles.

On the stone are two balls touching each other, and
under which is the following inscription in German:
„Anno MDCLXXXI. the XXII. January upon this spot
the Elector Charles unintentionally hit one ball against
the other which he fired out of one piece.“

Frederick V. under the charm of the illusory ideas
of his future happiness, did not dream of the reverses
of fortune which awaited his latter days. He had this
triumphal arch built in honour of his beloved sponse
and the beautiful garden laid out on the great rampart
of Louis V. He dreamed of his future sublime state,
clad in purple wearing a regal diadem, and died as a
fugitive his brow bound with the crown of thorns of
long-suffering. How beautifully true the poet A. VON
PLATEN expresses himself, when he says:

„Was lässt im Leben sich zuletzt gewinnen?
Was sichern wir von seinen Schätzen allen?
Das gold'ne Glück, das süsse Wohlgefallen,
Sie eilen — treu ist nur der Schmerz — von hinnen!“ [1])

---

[1]) „What at last do we gain in life?
What are the treasures we can make certain of?
A golden fortune, sweet pleasures,
They hasten fast away — nothing remains true to us but pain.“

The prospect from this garden is superb, we are struck with admiration in contemplating it. A grand picture unfolds itself to our sight, and shows us a charming tract of land full of cultivated fields, forests of fruit-trees, cut through by straight lines over which the steaming railway engine flies, like unto a dragon emitting fire, to join in its rapid flight both villages and towns. As if enveloped in transparent gauze, we see the towns of Ladenburg and Mannheim, to the left Schwetzingen with its celebrated garden, after having viewed all the wonders it contains, we cannot but think in spite of ourselves, that if Charles Theodore had laid out the enormous sums his liberality had lavished upon Schwetzingen in order to embellish Heidelberg, what extraordinary effects he might have produced there, where the great advantages of nature would have exacted so little effort from the aid of art. Certain it would be, that if the immense sums that have been expended upon those gardens had been laid out in the environs of Heidelberg castle, no other gardens in Europe could have competed with them.

But let us not speak of what might have been, but what is, and that in the vast districts of Germany, no mighty mortal hand could ever have formed upon a flat and even ground, a second spectacle so magnificent, however liberal and profuse might have been the riches of a prince so devoted a lover of the arts.

Look beneath our feet at the living panorama of our city of the muses, extending in its full length along the banks of the Neckar, which when gilded by the evening sun looks like a golden riband waving beautifully along on its way to join the mighty father Rhine that can be seen in its various windings glittering in the distance — then look further on into the back-ground and you will perceive the mountains of the Haardt bordered with a golden tint; at last cast up your eyes unto that splendid

96

azure canopy above, arched like a majestic dome above
this rich and sublime spectacle, and as the sun sets towards the west, encompasses it more and more with his
golden rays.

Really, wanderer, if, on a beautiful summer's evening,
thou enterest this enchanting garden of Elisabeth, thy
heart must be dilated with the sublime works of the
creation, and thou wilt feel the truth of Goethe's words
when he speaks of Heidelberg: „This town has in its
situation and in all its environs something of ideal
beauty" and exclaim with Schiller: „Ah! still how
beautiful is life!" [1])

To the friend of botany, our ruins offer a rich field
full of the most varied plants; even in April the yellow
wall-flower (*Cheiranthus Cheiri Lin.*) grows wild among
the fissures of the walls, and in the Elisabeth-garden
there is a most beautiful white linden-tree (*Tilia alba
Lin.*); near it rises majestically a large tulip-tree (*Lirio-
dendron tulipifera Lin.*) and close to the Elisabeth-gate
a majestic amyris (*Pinus balsamea Lin.*).

At the fountain of the princes, the wanderer will find
the Canadian bonduc or nickar-tree (*Gymnocladus cana-
densis Lam.*) and opposite to the blown-up tower the
purple oak tree (*Fagus sylvatica Lin. B. var. atropurpurea
Act.*). At the corner where the road leads to the tavern
we see a sugar-maple (*Acer saccharinum Lin.*); near the
bridge-house we find the flowery ash or manna ash tree
(*Fraxinus ornus*) and the *Ornus europaea*. At the corner
where the road leads to the lower fountain of the princes, and amongst the rose bushes near the tavern, as
well as in the principal path at the back are three *Salis-
burya adiantifolia Sm.* and on the lawn between the bridge-
house and the Elisabeth-gate there are two *Gleditschia
horrida W.* with their singular thorny shoots. On the

[1]) Posa in Schiller's Don Carlos.

old walls of the castle you will find the purple fox-glove (*Digitalis purpurea L.*), a poisonous plant, used in medicine. In the hedges and bushes of the castle is the common clematis or virgin's bower (*Clematis vitalba Lin.*) likewise a poisonous plant, and on the old walls the common worm-wood (*Artemisia absinthium L.*); the leaves of this poisonous plant are used in pharmacy; you will likewise find in the castle the common arum (*Arum vulgare Lin.*), the roots of which are also used medicinally.

In the Wolf's Cave (Wolfsschlucht) on the little Gaisberg above the castle stands the mountain alder (*Arnica montana L.*), both root and flowers are used medicinally.

The favorite woodroof (*Asperula odorata*) which gives so excellent a flavour to the May wine (wine infused with herbs), is frequently to be found in the neighbouring woods.

In the quarries of the Riesenstein (giant's stone) and the Gaisberg you will find the common bear's-foot (*Lycopodium clavatum L.*) the seeds of which are used in medicine. On the neighbouring mountains grows the common nightshade (*Atropa Belladonna Lin.*) its leaves and root are used in medicine, but its berries are poisonous.

In the forest belonging to the town of Heidelberg, the ground is almost covered with the common bilberry (*Vaccinium myrtillus Lin.*) and the adjacent heights are adorned with noble chesnut trees (*Castanea vesca E.*) in great quantities.

On the borders of the woods surrounding the castle and on sunny meadows you will find the *Orchis morio Lin.*, the *Orchis mascula L.*, the *Orchis maculata L.*, the broad-leaved (*Orchis latifolia L.*) and the helmet bladed (*Orchis militaris L.*), the roots of which are used in pharmacy. At the Haarlass the four-leaved true love (*Paris quadrifolia*) and in the whole of the surrounding neighbourhood in marshy places the bitter-sweet and deadly night-shade (*Solanum dulcamara L.*) is to be found.

With respect to zoology, it may be necessary to notice here, that many years ago, a redwinged wall-creeper or spider-catcher (Latham), was shot in the ruins of the castle, and such birds were afterwards repeatedly found again in the adjacent quarries. Over the Neckar, the osprey (*Pandion haliaëtos*) is to be seen hovering about in search of its prey, and the serpent or short-toed eagle (*Circaetos gallicus*) has been often shot from its eyry in the woods about Ziegelhausen. Amongst the rare phenomena of German ornithology, are the rose-coloured thrush (*Pastor roseus*), and the cream-coloured plover (*Cursor europaeus*); one specimen of each has been shot here.

What relates to the geognosy and geology of the environs of our castle, we cannot refer our readers to a better source than K. C. v. Leonhard's excellent work on Heidelberg [1]) which says that there is to be found near the town sand, gravel, rubblestone, luss, shell-lime-stone and variegated sandstone, and next to these nep-tunian formations, the plutonian mountain qualities appear, such as granite and fieldstone-porphyry. The sandstone of the Gaisberg has for a long time furnished most excellent materials for building; it is exported both far and wide, and its durability is the cause of its great success.

---

[1]) Mr. von Leonhard gives in his work upon Heidelberg most interesting notices upon the vegetable and animal world of our neighbourhood, for which he is indebted to the well known professor of natural history, the aulic counsellor BRONN. Our readers, who wish to instruct themselves further in the Flora of the neighbourhood, we will refer them to the Flora Heidelbergensis of the late botanist BISCHOFF (Heidelberg, C. Groos), and to the newest work of professor SCHMIDT (Heidelberg, Mohr 1857). For the above notices of the flora of the castle and its environs, the editor of this work has to thank Mr. LANG, gardener to the university.

The oldest granites, says von Leonhard, are coarser grained, which by crystal feldspar being frequently dispersed over the whole mass, receive a kind of texture of porphyry. The new granites are known by the turmelins about them that almost never fail; others contain small red garnets, and likewise, but seldomer, pinite, beryl &c.

The granite near the castle only rises to the height of 635 feet above the surface of the sea, upon which the red sand-stone lies that is dug out of the several quarries of the Gaisberg and the Königsstuhl (King's seat). — One of the most interesting objects of the whole vicinity in regard to geognosy, is to be found in the castle ditch, near the lower Prince's Fountain, where the layer of sandstone is perceptible on the granite. The sandstone near the steep side of the rock, to the left of the fish pond behind the Castle tavern, is entirely composed of fragments of porphyry.

I shall now conclude this part, having a few words to add about the arrangement of the gardens of old castles in general, and refer principally to the German Arts-Journal of Mr. Jäger, N° 13, Series of 1853, who says:

„Since the old Castle of VEITSBURG is restored under the name of RHEINSTEIN, and the new HOHENSCHWANGAU with its marble rocks near the summits of the high Alps, so beautifully reflected in the waters of the blue Schwansee (Swan lake), in all parts of Germany old castles rise out of their ruins in new pomp and splendour, and shine again far out into the wide land as in olden times.

But as these castles are inhabited from time to time, it is natural that the arrangements around the buildings should be laid out with taste. I cannot decide whether the architects employed to reconstruct these castles, have judged of their nearest environs in a higher artistical point of view, or if they have here taken the same liberties as in the apartments destined to be inhabited, and have only considered the modern luxury with which the present inhabitants so much desire to surround them. The modern gardens and plantations in most of the restored castles, seem to confirm this.

It may be that the plantations in the most of them were left entirely to the judgment of the gardener, who, although he might have been an artist in his way, had before him an unknown ground, and consequently did not fail to introduce such usual modern forms, as are seen in other castles, and more particularly, in the numerous lordly castellated country manor-houses in England, showing all those modern innovations and even having greenhouses attached to them.

That is a great error, which unfortunately has been too often committed, and it is now time to endeavour to enlighten ourselves on this subject, and try upon what principle similar plantations might be laid out, in order to harmonize in a worthy manner with those majestic works of architecture, and to form an artistical conception as the basis."

The Editor continues to remark that the plantations of such gardens should, to fulfil the task conscientiously, be in perfect harmony with the style and character of the edifices of the middle-age, in order to pretend to any intellectual merit, and to elevate the impression of the whole.

This is also the wish of the high and sovereign authorities, and I consider it my honest duty to fulfil it strictly; consequently our Castle plantation will no longer be a modern artificial garden, but one in perfect unison with the venerable Castle with its old walls and its environs endowed with so rich a nature. The old trees corresponding with the old walls shall be carefully preserved, and new branches of them planted worthy of the Castle for the future.

May a careful watch be taken at all times that this task be observed, and put into execution in a manner worthy of the whole: this is the wish and desire of the Editor of this work, who, as far as ever it lies in his power, and no obstacles be laid in his way, will do his utmost to see that this task be faithfully executed.

In order to render the work more complete for the inquisitive wanderer, we shall, in the second part, proceed with the description of the most interesting places in the immediate environs of Heidelberg.

PART II.

—

WANDERINGS

TO THE

ENVIRONS OF HEIDELBERG CASTLE.

I. WANDERING.

WOLFSBRUNNEN (Wolf's Fountain), DRACHENHÖHLE (Dragon's
Cave), SCHLIERBACH, ZIEGELHAUSEN, STIFT NEUBURG
and HAARLASS.

Du edler Brunnen Du mit Ruh' und Lust umgeben,
Mit Bergen hier und da als einer Burg umringt,
Prinz aller schönen Quell, aus welchem Wasser dringt,
Anmuthiger denn Milch und köstlicher denn Reben,
Da uns'res Landes Kron' und Haupt mit seinem Leben
Der werthen Nimph' oft selbst die lange Zeit verbringt,
Da das Geflügel ihr zu Ehren lieblich singt,
Da nur Ergötzlichkeit und keusche Wollust schweben,
Vergeblich bist Du nicht in dieses grüne Thal
Beschlossen vom Gebirg' und Klippen überall:
Die köstliche Natur hat darum Dich umfangen
Mit Felsen und Gebüsch, auf dass man wissen soll
Dass alle Fröhlichkeit sei Müh' und Arbeit voll
Und dass auch nichts so schön es sei schwer zu erlangen.

So sung MARTIN OPITZ [1]) the Father of German
poetry, under the shade of the old lime-trees, when
he studied at the University of Heidelberg more than
two centuries ago; the charms of this delicious spring
had ever inspired him, and after the old bard, the delights of this charming and shady fountain have been
sung innumerable times up to the present hour.

Lafontaine chose this spot as a place of meeting

---

[1]) The Poet Martin Opitz who has been rightly called the Father
of German poetry, he having first opened the path, was born at
Bunzlau in Silesia in 1597 and died of the plague at Dantzig the
20th August 1639. This poet studied at Heidelberg in 1619, when
the University was in its prime.

for truly feeling souls in his Clara du Plessis and her faithful Clairant, and still in our days crowds of young lovers wander to this place, and many a vow has been sworn to eternity, that alas! too often the ensuing spring had already dissolved. — The majestic lime-trees that formerly shaded this spring have fallen under the axe, and so this charming spot has been deprived of one of its most beautiful ornaments.

The poet and historian ALOIS SCHREIBER complains of these shady lime-trees having been cut down, in the following words:

„Alas! they have destroyed those trees that once shaded the sacred brow of the poet! They say, that they were injurious to the trout in the ponds; so it is thus we wantonly destroy what is beautiful, to procure ourselves a good dish of fish and a few cords of wood!"

Deeply concealed in the little friendly valley, lies the celebrated and well-known Wolf's Fountain, and many romantic traditions on its subject are still preserved in the recollection of the people.

It is related that JETTA, the wife of the Franconian Prince ANTHYSUS who lived in a mansion on the same spot where now the magnificent ruins of the Heidelberg Castle stand, often foretold in a chapel of her mansion, of the future splendour that would embellish that hill, and that the arts and sciences would erect their seat of the Muses down in the valley on the banks of the Neckar; but one day as she was wandering near the spring, which since then has been called the Wolf's Fountain, she was attacked by a she-wolf and torn to pieces.

The delicious trout preserved here in several ponds in the form of terraces one above the other, are much renowned on account of their delicate flavour, and generally form the principal feature in the gastronomic bill of fare, so that they are often sent as far as Frankfort on the Maine. The road that leads from the

Castle to the Wolf's Fountain is delightful, and will only take the wanderer half an hour to walk; the view from there over the Valley of the Neckar, the Stift Neuburg (convent of Neuburg) and the village of Ziegelhausen reminds one very much of the Swiss landscapes. This was the favorite spot of many of the Electors and their consorts, who often frequented it, and which Father OPITZ often mentions in his poetry.

The lover of wild romantic spots has only to ascend the mountain from the Wolf's-Brunnen a little further along the new road already mentioned, when he will come to a mass of rocks grotesquely heaped together which would have furnished ample matter for the pencil of a Salvator Rosa; this place in called the Drachenhöhle (Dragon's cave).

Then, respected wanderer, when thou hast partaken of the delicious trout and refreshed thyself with some of the worthy host's good wine, go further and follow me along the little trout-stream, thou wilt see to the left the opening of a passage almost filled up; it probably was in former times a conduit, and the people now call it the „Pagan's cave."

From here we pass the mill of our gay and worthy host of the Wolf's Fountain Mr. Leitz, down to old Schlierbach, a little hamlet, now belonging to Heidelberg, but much older than that town.

Before we continue our description further, let us return to the Journal of Frederick IV. that we have already mentioned, for it is said therein of the Wolf's Fountain: that not only he and his illustrious predecessors liked to pass their time in this spot, but that it had been for many years before and after, the favorite place for the principal parties of pleasure of the inhabitants of Heidelberg, and that the professors of the University often gave entertainments there to their friends.

He further relates, under the date of 26th May 1598:

„we fished at the Wolf's Fountain", and on the 13th June of the same year „we dined there." And further very ingenuously says, on the 9th June, „I got drunk there."

We have again to thank the city of Heidelberg for the construction of a new road, which on ascending a little higher than that leading from the Molkenkur to the upper Dragon's cave, and the Wolf'sbrunnen, brings you through a bed of rocks, where, to the right and left, thousands of colossal rocks like ruins surround you, and which involuntarily draw forth the admiration of the astonished traveller.

Like the Wolf's Fountain, so at that time old Schlierbach was much frequented; for in Frederick the Fourth's day-book he says, on the 31st May 1598, „we ate a pike at SCHLIERBACH." From here we can proceed to Heidelberg on a most beautiful road along the Neckar, where to our left the houses of Schlierbach seem to cling to the masses of granite which every moment appear to threaten their destruction; but we will pursue our course on the road to Neckargemünd on the left bank of the Neckar, till we cross the ferry opposite to ZIEGELHAUSEN, and arrive, after trusting ourselves to the mercy of the floods of the river, at this village, the situation of which is extremely picturesque. It is there where the Reverend professor SCHMETZER resides, so well known and deservedly celebrated by the several popular and scientific works he has written, and we shall likewise find in the catholic curate of the village a most worthy man of very profound erudition.

Ziegelhausen is of much later origin than that of the many villages in the neighbourhood of Heidelberg, for it is not mentioned in any of the old annals. It owes its existence, as its name indicates, to a manufactory of tiles or a brick-kiln, that belonged to the convent of Schönau, two leagues distance from there, situated in a charming valley surrounded by a beautiful forest.

The village has most excellent meadows, where the inhabitants of Mannheim and Heidelberg send their linen to be bleached; the STEINBACH flows through it and is well furnished with trout. Its picturesque situation we have already described. From here we reach the foot of the hill on which lies the collegiate foundation or CONVENT of NEUBURG (Stift Neuburg).

A certain ANSCHELM transformed an ancient castle here into a monastery in 1048, and dedicated its church to St. Berthold; but under CONRAD of HOHENSTAUFEN, Neuburg became a convent or an establishment for young ladies of rank, of which the eldest daughter of CONRAD, CUNIGUNDA, was the first abbess, and where, for many centuries, noble ladies were brought up and educated in virtue and piety, and so formed to become chaste spouses worthy of ancient German manners. Later, when the convent became degenerated, it was suppressed and in the XVII. century added to the electoral domains. The Elector JOHN WILLIAM presented it to the Jesuits in 1709, after the dissolution of this order it was occupied by the Lazarists, then finally became the property of the catholic church, when it was sold to a layman.

The present proprietress of this really charming possession is Madame SCHLOSSER, relict of the late counsellor of that name. The romantic plantations and the beautiful waterfall may be visited on returning from the excellent inn of the Stiftsmühle (the mill of the foundation) a house worthy to be recommended. The wanderer will be thoroughly recompensed for his walk, for the worthy Lady of the manor, possesses most amiable qualities, and is always willing to grant to every respectable visitor the permission of walking over this really fairy estate.

In the year 1833 a very interesting gravestone was found here in a pond belonging to the estate, but the inscription was wanting; it represented in demi-relief a

lady, on one side of which were to be seen the arms
of the Margraves of Baden and on the other those of
the Palatinate. It is supposed that under this stone
BEATRICE, the daughter of Margrave CHRISTOPHER I.
of Baden, wife of JOHN II., Palsgrave of Simmern, was
buried, and who died in 1535.

At the foot of the hill of the foundation, is the mill
surrounded with immensely tall poplars, where the wanderer can procure refreshments. A part of the church
is likewise restored to its former service, and the windows ornamented with several beautiful glass paintings.

Not far from the Stift Neuburg we arrive at the
Haarlass — now a very large tannery, belonging to the
ancient Burgomaster SPEYERER, a worthy man, who not
only as first Burgomaster of Heidelberg has obtained
the esteem of all his fellow citizens, but likewise rendered the state much service as an independent Deputy of
its Chambers. Tradition says that in former times a
chapel was erected on this spot, where those virgins,
who entered the convent of Neuburg as nuns, were deprived of their hair, the principal ornament of their head,
hence its name of HAARLASS; which means „HAIRLESS"
(but that could not have been the case, for this ceremony was always performed in the convent - church).
Later there was an inn here belonging to the foundation,
but now converted by Mr. Speyerer, independent of the
tannery, into a beautiful country-house, and the traveller
who visits the charming plantation immediately above this
establishment, will enjoy a most magnificent prospect.

A truly romantic walk above the „Haarlass" leading
through colossal masses of granite rocks has been laid
out by the artist BERNHARD FRIES, a worthy brother of
the painter FRIES, mentioned in the following page.

From here it is only half an hour's walk to Heidelberg.

II. WANDERING.

THE MONUMENT OF THE PAINTER ERNEST FRIES, MOL-
KENKUR (Whey-cure Establishment), RÖMERWEG (Roman road),
KÖNIGSSTUHL (King's seat), SPEYERERHOF, three projecting
forts called: DEFIANCE TO THE BAVARIAN, DEFIANCE TO
THE EMPEROR and DEFIANCE TO THE PRIEST (the Pope),
the WATERFALL, the BRUNNENSTOLLEN and the KLINGEN-
TEICH.

We shall begin our second wandering from the castle-
garden, turn to the right near the upper fountain of the
princes, where passing along a shady path through a
door made in an old wall, and ascending some steps,
reach a very well constructed road that to the left leads
to the Molkenkur, and to the right, but rather steep,
up to the Königsstuhl. But as we have already visited
the former place, turn to the right, and if we are on
foot take a very agreeable and broad road, which may
also be ascended with asses, then turn round and soon
arrive at a spot near a mass of rocks of variegated
sandstone, which presents to the eye a most picturesque
group. This road was constructed by the late director
of the garden, METZGER, and called in honour of the
painter FRIES the „Friesenweg" (Fries's road). A cavern
found in this road, was called the Jetta-cavern, but
has no historical authority for that appellation; the
most interesting object in it is the tablet hewn in the
rock to the memory of the painter ERNEST FRIES, to
whom art and his friends have paid their tribute of
regret for his premature death; it recalls to our memory

one of those most distinguished landscape - painters of
his time; he preferred frequenting this spot of all others,
for it was here as a boy he first began his studies in
the art.

Inclosed within a simple border you may read the
following inscription:

DEM MALER
ERNST FRIES
DIE
BEWOHNER HEIDELBERGS
UND
SEINE FREUNDE
MDCCCXLI

To the painter Ernest Fries, the inhabitants of Heidelberg and his friends, 1841.

In the prime of his life, death deprived the world
of this man of rare talents. Heidelberg reckons among
her sons many more talented artists, of whom ERNEST
FRIES, CHARLES FOHR and ROTTMANN are dead; the
genial Mr. von LEONHARD whom we have often before
mentioned, speaks several times in his guide book on
the subject of these artists:

„The celebrated artists with their indisputable talent,
at first devoted their juvenile productions to their native
town and its environs."

„It is evident from a judgement of Goethe, that the
eye accustoms and forms itself to those objects, which
it has seen in its infancy, and consequently Venetian
painters must see in a livelier and clearer light than
other men, so we should consider ourselves right in

admitting, that what connoisseurs praise in the paintings of Fries and of Fohr, to paint nature without idealizing her, without imaginative ornament, seizing alone her intensive grandeur as a subject of artistical production — we should consider ourselves right, I say — in connecting the rare genius bestowed upon those deceased artists with the impressions that were first made upon their young minds in the environs of their native town."

We now reach a delightful road, shaded with chesnut trees on the top of the little Gaisberg, on which, as we have already stated in our historical introduction the old Heidelberg castle was built. Nothing but the remains of the Roman road which led to the old castle and further up — now called the „Plättlisweg" (paved road), remind us of those remote times, and of which we know so little. The old fort all traces of which have long since disappeared, was built upon the foundations of a Roman castle, and the accounts we have of it refer back to the second and third century of the christian aera. This castle was in connection with one built on the left bank of the Neckar (Wasserburg), on the spot where the building for the royal stables in Heidelberg now stands, which confirms what KREUTZER says, that the Romans were wont to cover all the outlets of their mountain defiles with forts and entrenchments according to the principles of their strategy. From this castle (Wasserburg) a paved road — the above mentioned Plättlisweg — for pedestrians and riders, led to the castle on the little Gaisberg, and from there, further up to the Königsstuhl and Gaiberg (Gowinbrech), celebrated for its excellent cherries, besides this road likewise leads to other Roman mountain castles DILSBERG and STEINSBERG into Wurtemberg. These were Roman military roads, which at that time formed the only ways of communication, for then no road had been made through the rugged valley of the Neckar. Later a broad and almost straight road conducted from the old castle on the little Gaisberg to the Wolfsbrunnen; but let us cast our looks from the past to the present time, and we shall have at our feet almost a bird's eye view of the magnificent castle we are now acquainted with in all its details, the whole of which now presents itself before us. We are struck with a particular feeling when we look down upon all these different buildings and recall to our mind those past days of joy and sorrow, so that we might exclaim with the poet:

„Ja, ich fühle hier dein Wehen, heilige Vergangenheit,
  Um mich schweben ungesehen Geister aus der Heldenzeit."

„Yes, I feel here the gentle breezes of those sacred times that are past,
And the invisible spirits of thy heroic age hover round about me."

Towns and villages lie before us at our feet, and far beyond the ancient city of Worms, we can trace the windings of the majestic Rhine. Opposite to us on the other side of the Neckar is the HEILIGENBERG with its sunny hills, formerly the seat of a reputed monastery.

It was in this Castle situated on a rock, the last ruins of which have almost totally disappeared, that the Count Palatine LOUIS II., surnamed the Severe, died in 1294 and who out of blind jealousy had his wife beheaded in the same room in which he was born. In 1537 the tower of the old Castle of Heidelberg that contained the powder, was set on fire by lightning and burnt this old castle, which had already suffered much by fire in 1278, entirely to the ground.

Ancient chronicles of those times relate of it as follows:

„On the 25th of April 1537, a terrible darkness arose accompanied with thick clouds and a furious raging of the winds, after which a most terrible thunderstorm broke out and the lightning struck a tower of the old castle containing powder, saltpetre and other combustibles of war, and set it on fire; by the force of the explosion the old edifice was rent and burnt to the ground, and all around trembled as if it had been shaken by an earthquake. In the town innumerable window-panes were broken, doors lifted from their hinges, and the inhabitants were in fear of the total destruction of the town, and the approach of the day of judgment. Huge stones were precipitated into the town, destroying the houses, wounding and killing many of the inhabitants, who out of fear were escaping from their houses. Two children of a man living in the old castle were killed, and five others seriously injured; in the new castle the Elector's apartment was so shattered and destroyed, that if the prince Louis V. had been in it at the time, he could not have escaped without having been in danger of his life."

A certain Mr. Wagner had the fortunate idea of erecting on the spot of the old castle an establishment for the Whey cure, which from its charming situation is much frequented by the strangers and inhabitants; but on ascending higher we shall have a more extensive view from the Königsstuhl [1]).

If, respected wanderer, you are a good climber, let us now take the roman road and ascend the mountain till you reach the back [2]), from where a straight road leads through a forest of larch trees covered with moss, to the foot of the beautiful tower erected by the Grand-Duke LEOPOLD in 1832.

---

[1]) It is interesting to know that there is a spring in the north-west direction of the highest point of the Königsstuhl, called the Stock-brunnen, which formerly emptied its abundant supply of water out of two large pipes, but is at present closed, the water being now conducted from there to the Speierhof.

[2]) A very commodious carriage road and not very steep, likewise conducts you there along the quarry; it takes more time to reach the top of the Königsstuhl, but the road is not so fatiguing.

A little to the north of the tower is a small house, where the fatigued tourist may repose and in fine weather procure refreshments; an excellent telescope is kept here, through which the most distant objects may be distinctly seen; a hundred and forty steps lead to the top of the tower, from whence you can enjoy a most magnificent view of the whole of the surrounding country.

The height of the mountain according to Munke is 1752 feet, according to Lokhardt 1687 and according to others even 1800 feet above the level of the sea. Its name is of ancient origin, and PAULUS MELISSUS relates in 1598 that there is a mountain above the castle called the „Königsstuhl“ (King's seat) on the top of which was an old oak with large extending branches, and under its shade seats were erected; it is not at all improbable that in ancient times this was a sacred spot, and was the place where the elections of the Carlovingian and Saxon emperors took place &c.

However M. de LEONHARD says, according to a relation of the Pastor ZÜLLIG: It is to be remarked, that on many of the mountains of Germany on their highest elevation, there is a bare isolated stone or rock of a large size and imposing appearance, which looks as if it were intended for the seat of a king, who held his council there, while the nobles of his court or the chiefs of the tribes were seated upon lower stones or upon the earth round about him. So it is with the King's seat on the Mont-tonnerre on the other side of the Rhine, that of the Fichtelgebirge (the Pine mountains) on the Island of Rügen, and others. This induced me some years ago to see if such a seat was not to be found on the top of our Königsstuhl, and which perhaps eventually has given its name to the whole mountain. On the front or that side looking towards the town, i. e. on the highest part of the mountain, nothing of the kind was to be discovered; but on the north-east declivity, I was led into the road up to the Königsstuhl, and was shown the king's stone, well known to the sportsmen of the neighbourhood; it is a block of sandstone 13½ feet in length, 4 in breadth and rising above the earth to about 2¾ feet.

From the front top of the mountain the mass of rocks is about half a league distant, opposite to Ziegel-hausen above the farm „Leuthof" on the so-called green lawn. It is not the question here, as upon other mountains, of a mighty towering rock, but it has some resemblance though small to such a royal seat situated on a mountain.

This denomination for isolated masses of rocks must have been very common amongst the ancient Germans, and may perhaps have extended to less important analogies, so that there is no hesitation of this name having been made use of for the Königsstuhl, and afterwards for the forest in which it is situated, and gradually at last to designate the whole height of the broad back of the mountain to the opening of the valley. The view presented to the tourist from the top of the tower is sublime beyond description.

From Mayence, Worms, Mannheim and Spires, he will on looking to the south perceive the tower of the Strasburg Minster, like a pyramid surrounded with a transparent mist; opposite to him, the blue mountains of the Haardt, and to his right the woody heights of the Odenwald; to the south-east he will perceive the mountains of Suabia, which join those of Baden-Baden towards the south. When you have, my respected wanderer, fully enjoyed this magnificent sight, and beheld all the interesting objects visible from this spot, cast a look, after descending, upon this slender yet strong built tower. The foundation stone of the tower was laid in October 1832, and on that occasion the inhabitants of Heidelberg and the neighbourhood celebrated a

118

public festival on the spot. Manuscripts, coins, and
the finest juice of the grape, were according to old
custom deposited therein, were they will most likely
remain for ages to come.

The merit of the first idea of erecting a tower upon
this mountain is ascribed to a bookseller of Hessen-
Cassel a certain Mr. Jacobi.

The stone tablet over the entrance bears the following inscription:

DEM GENUSSE SCHOENER NATUR
DER GROSSHERZOG LEOPOLD
DIE BEWOHNER HEIDELBERGS
UND FREUNDE AUS NAEHE UND FERNE.
MDCCCXXXII — XXXV.

„For the enjoyment of beautiful nature,
The Grand-Duke Leopold
The Inhabitants of Heidelberg
And Friends from far and near.
1832 — 35.“

In 1815 the Emperors Francis of Austria and
Alexander of Russia ascended this mountain, and in
consequence the people changed the name of Königsstuhl
into Kaisersstuhl (Emperor's seat). A stone now covered
with brambles marks this event, by an inscription to
posterity.

Let us now return to the carriage road. We leave
to the right a footpath which descends by steps to the
castle in a straight direction toward the north, called
Himmelsleiter (Heaven's ladder), and follow the road
along the back of the mountain; a little further on we
leave this road also to the right, where we shall soon
arrive at the Speierer-Hof situated about 400 feet lower
than the Königsstuhl. The town of Heidelberg let out
on lease about 113 acres of forestland for cultivation
and gave to this new farm the name of its ancient
Burgomaster Speierer, and whom we have already

mentioned, in consideration of the many services he had
rendered to the town. A very respectable inn and
worthy to be recommended is attached to the farm;
when you have arrived at this spot, if the view is not
so very striking, you are still delighted with the charming repose of the forest, the fresh and soft verdure of
the meadows and the woods, and the rich and beautiful
varieties of the truly romantic road which leads from
here to Heidelberg. If you should wish to prolong
your walk, you may go on as far as the Bierhälderhof ¹), through a lively little valley, interspersed with
brooks and mills, and at the foot of the declivity of the
mountain is situated the ancient village of ROHRBACH,
which from the quantity of roman antiquities that have
been found there, seems to indicate its having been
formerly the site of a roman colony.

The Prince of Deux-Ponts the magnanimous MAXI-
MILIAN JOSEPH, afterwards King of Bavaria, lived with
the whole of his family during the great french Revolution in the little castle of Rohrbach, and later when
he ascended the throne of Bavaria, he made a present
of this country-seat to his illustrious mother-in-law the
late Margravine AMELIA of BADEN, who often passed
the summer there in quiet rural repose, in the sweet and
noble pleasure of doing good, and dispensing her charity
to all the poor of the neighbourhood. We will now
however continue our route along the beautiful high
road to Heidelberg, constructed by the town at a great
expence. We shall then soon arrive at the classical
spot where FREDERICK I., the Victorious set up his

¹) From the Bierhälderhof at a little distance from the road to
Rohrbach, to the right of the projecting land, is a terrace planted with
trees, called CARLSLUST, which a Duke CHARLES of Deux-Ponts se-
lected on account of its extensive and really beautiful prospect as a
favorite place of resort, and which he frequented on fine mornings in
his walks from Rohrbach.

triple defiance in the following manner: „Defiance to the Bavarian, defiance to the Emperor and defiance to the Priest (the Pope)." Of these outworks, to which may be added a star- and half-moon redoubt erected to cover the town and the castle, are only here and there a few ruins of the walls, but the memory of their first founder, rightly called the Victorious, will live as long as history remains, for he came victorious out of all his battles, enlarged his country, and increased his treasury.

It is related of him, when building these outworks, that he assembled the whole of his council to announce to them the approaching war, and gave them a detailed account of his available military forces, whereupon they, fearing his mighty adversaries, did all in their power to dissuade him from the undertaking; but this valiant prince replied: „though we know full well that your meaning is good, you must however know, that it is not the question now — whether we must go to war? I will not charge your conscience with the question whether I will or not; for that depends on me to wage war; I know beforehand what danger may befal me, and it is I that have decided. You may always get another master if you are driven from without our country, but we cannot so easily get another country if they drive me out of it."

In another old work we find the following tale: FREDERICK Elector and Palsgrave of the Rhine, surnamed the Victorious having lost his way during the chase, and coming with his horse to the edge of a rocky precipice, an old woman, occupied in picking up some sticks, saw the danger in which her beloved sovereign was, and in her ardent zeal the woman cried out: „Couldst thou not find another road, has the devil led thee up so high? well, may God help thee in coming down again."

Frederick immediately checking his restive horse, turned round and rode up to the furious woman. He asked her, „if she knew to whom she was speaking, and if she did, why she had the boldness to address him thus?" — „To be sure I know", said she, „that thou art our Elector, and thou art in war with all the world; if thy temerity cost thee thy life, if thou fall'st with thy horse down over the cliff into the deep vale beneath, who will suffer more, than thy poor country? If thou wilt not spare thyself, spare at least thy poor subjects." „Thou art right Dame", replied the victorious prince smiling and throwing his purse to the old woman said, „I will do so no more."

Further along the road we enjoy a beautiful view from the so-called Kanzel (the Pulpit) — and see beneath our feet masses of gigantic rocks which have fallen from a higher declivity, the largest of these blocks is called the Riesenstein (Giant's stone) and lies 652 feet above the level of the sea.

The large quarries to the right are also very interesting. Now we shall arrive at another new creation of Heidelberg, an artificial waterfall, but the principal thing we have to regret about it is, that the greatest part of the year the water is wanting — but after a few days rain this artificial cascade presents a very pretty aspect.

It may perhaps be of interest to many of our readers to notice here a stoll or water-feeder which is hewn deep into the rock and very probably may have served formerly to supply the castle with water.

We will now lead our wanderer further along this agreeable walk by the Klingenteich to Heidelberg.

III. WANDERING

THROUGH THE ENVIRONS OF THE CASTLE OF HEIDELBERG.

THE NECKAR-BRIDGE, HIRSCHGASSE, PHILOSOPHENWEG
(Philosopher's walk), MICHELSBERG and HEILIGENBERG;
HANDSCHUCHSHEIM, NEUENHEIM.

We shall begin our third walk over the handsome
bridge of the Neckar, where we must rest awhile to
notice the lively traffic on the river below us; at times
we may perceive the immense rafts floating down into
the Rhine the riches of the woods of the Odenwald and
the Black forests, at times heavy laden barges trans-
porting goods from the busy trading town of Heilbronn
to Mannheim, a town now flourishing with increasing
splendour, or behold the poor weary horses dragging
along the craft up the river through the arches of the
bridge, patiently suffering under the whip of the drivers,
or contemplate the rippling of the waves and call to
our mind the words of Tanner:

> „Eine Welle sprach zur Andern:
> Ach wie kurz ist doch das Wandern,
> Und die Zweite sprach zur Dritten:
> Kurz gelebt heisst kurz gelitten!"

> Said a wave to another in active sport,
> Alas! our wanderings here how short!
> To a third wave the last made this reply,
> We all suffer less, when early we die.

Göthe also expresses himself at the sight of this
bridge in saying:

„The bridge shows itself in such beauty, perhaps not to be equalled by any bridge in the world; through its arches you see the Neckar flowing down to the flat plains of the Rhine, and beyond that river in the distance the lovely blue mountains on its opposite bank. To the right a ruddy coloured rock covered with verdure and joining itself to the multitude of vineyards, closes the prospect."

The late historian and Aulic Counsellor ALOIS SCHREIBER reports that in 1288 there were two bridges over the Neckar, the first where the present one now stands, and the second between Neuenheim and Bergheim. The latter gave way and fell down in the same year, just as a procession was going over, and more than 300 persons fell into the river and were drowned. After the former wooden bridges, that were erected in place of the present one, were destroyed, either by the war or the drifting of the ice, the beautiful structure we now admire was begun in 1786 and completed in 1788; it is 700 feet long and 30 feet broad and built of the strong red sandstone from the neighbouring quarries. According to the inscription on the gate of the bridge, it was constructed under the direction of the privy-councellor VON BABO, by the architect Majer of Mannheim; more than 200 men are said to have been employed daily in its construction. Two tolerably fine statues, well executed, though in bad taste by Link, sculptor to the court, adorn the bridge. The one near the bridge gate on the side of the town represents CHARLES THEODORE, surrounded by the figures of the native rivers, the Rhine, the Danube, the Neckar and the Moselle; the other towards the north, Minerva, the Goddess of Wisdom, at her feet the symbolic figures of Faith, Science, Commerce and Agriculture. — Sad remembrances are attached to this bridge, for in the year 1799 the Austrians and the

French fought a bloody battle here. The French, far superior in number were beaten back seven times by 200 Hungarian infantry and 80 lancers, were forced to leave the place of action, and did not return to it till the next morning after the little band of heroes had left the same in the dead of the night. It is said that much blood was shed here, and that an immense number of the French were either killed by the grape shot of the Austrians, or found their graves in the waters of the Neckar; there is also mention of the brave act of a french drummer, worthy of being committed to posterity.

Beating to the assault, the drummer scarce beyond the age of boyhood advanced to meet the enemy, and when a ball had shattered his leg, leaning against the parapet of the bridge, he still continued beating his march. On which one of the enemy's officers is said to have dismounted from his horse, and slung a drum across his shoulders, and beat it to animate the courage of his soldiers. There are still to be seen at the gate of the bridge and at some of the mutilated parts of the statues, traces of the destruction of that period. Also in 1849 during the Baden revolution, the bridge was threatened to be destroyed, for the insurgents had already undermined it, in order to spring it up on the approach of the Prussians, and we have only to owe its preservation to the courageous resistance of several citizens of Heidelberg. After having related the events which are attached to this bridge, and delighted our eye with the beautiful panorama which surrounds us, let us direct our steps along the beautiful villas on the other side towards the Hirschgasse (Stag's path), a place of amusement, but which has already seen a great deal of bloodshed; for in a room to the left in the Inn there, and which bears the same name, the students of Heidelberg settle their disputes, which often terminate very sadly, and which has often proved of serious consequence to a promising student on whom perhaps an aged parent had fixed his hopes, and perhaps had been thus deprived of his only son and future support through life.

From there let us ascend the hill a little to the so-called Philosopher's walk (Philosophenweg) a carriage road, from where you have a most beautiful and varied prospect over the romantic valley of the Neckar, the castle in front of the Königsstuhl, the Molkenkur, the valley of the Rhine far beyond Spires, and towards the south as well as the west, the horizon is bounded by the rugged mountains of the Vosges and the Haardt. We are now upon a part of the Heiligenberg, a mountain 1300 feet above the level of sea, and formerly called *Mons pius* by the Romans; then we continue our route still ascending to the left through a shady wood, and come to the ruins of the church of St. Michael, near to which there is a hole known by the name of the Pagan's Hole. — It is said that formerly under the Emperor VALENTINIAN 370 years after Christ, there was a roman fort built here and a temple dedicated to the Gods, and the Pagan's hole above mentioned to have been an Oracle, from where the idol gave its answers through these pagan holes already related, by means of vaulted passages leading down to the Neckar. [1]

According to ancient traditions, the Franconian Kings constructed at a later period a palace on the remains of the roman fort, called „Abrinisburg“, and at that time the whole of the mountain went by the name of „Abraham's mount“ (Abrahamsberg). On the summit of the mountain the ruins of the Abbey of the Heiligenberg are still to be seen, it was inhabited by monks of the Benedictine order from the monastery of

---

[1] According to Leger, this pagan hole was nothing more than a reservoir for water hewn into the rock.

LORSCH, and from the extent of these ruins, one may judge of the former size and splendour of this religious edifice [1]) of which a poet says: „Where are now the days when thou wast seen shining in thy splendour; where thy vaulted arches; where the sacred incense that filled thy vast halls, and the choir that resounded with the sacred hymns of praises unto the Lord? Gone, all gone! Ruins surround me! these dark remains announce nought but sorrow. The song has ceased, and only the plaintive cry of the screech-owl disturbs the dead silence. Has the blade of ATTILA made all this havoc? Or hast thou CHRONOS, murderer of thy children, destroyed that which formerly thy mighty arm created? Or has presumption ravaged this sacred spot? GOD, JEHOVAH and ALLAH are they not One, though sounding differently unto the ear? "

In the thirty-years' war the stones of the church of St. Michael were made use of to erect forts. TILLY took them, and bombarded (from the church of St. Michael) the town of Heidelberg in 1622, but was driven back from his position by the besieged. From the Heiligenberg a footpath leads through the little valley of the SEVEN MILLS to the ancient village of HANDSCHUCHSHEIM, already known in the time of SIPIUS, King of the Franks, and in the church of this large village, dedicated to St. Nazarin, were found many interesting tombstones, mostly belonging to the noble family of Handschuchsheim, or as they were then called „HENTSCHUSHEIM", and who already appear in the twelfth century as noble vassals of the Convent of LORSCH; particular attention is due, amongst these numerous monuments, to the statues of a Lord of Handschuchsheim, his wife and two children. The vaults of the Lords of Hand-

---

[1]) If the cultivation of the valley of the Neckar did not alone proceed from the Benedictine Monks of the Heiligenberg they at least contributed to it most materially.

schuchsheim are easily to be known by their coat of arms, a glove argent in azure field.

The last Lord of the race of Handschuchsheim, John, a youth of sixteen, quarrelled at a wedding (1600) with Frederick de Hirschhorn, and a duel took place in which JOHN de HANDSCHUCHSHEIM was so seriously wounded that he expired soon after; his old mother became quite disconsolable at the loss of her only son and last scion of this ancient race; it caused her to utter terrible imprecations on the house of Hirschhorn, at that time blessed with many promising children, and not long after the numerous heirs of FREDERICK de HIRSCHHORN were carried off by epidemic diseases and such like distempers, till even Frederick himself, now the last of his race, was buried in his tomb with his shield. The estates of the Handschuchsheims now came to the family of HELMSTÄDT who are still in possession of several of them. Of the castles of Handschuchsheim, there is only one remaining, the property of the family of Helmstädt, the construction of which is very interesting. ALOIS SCHREIBER relates that in the archives of this family were found accounts of a secret tribunal that was held here. The ecclesiastical counsellor Mühling (Curate and Dean of Handschuchsheim) likewise relates that nearly 80 years ago, a nobleman then on a visit to Mr. de Helmstädt had struck against the wall on descending a winding staircase with the master of the house, and upon the wall sounding hollow, the proprietor of the castle immediately sent for a mason, who was working in the neighbourhood, to make a breach in the wall at that spot, when a skeleton in complete armour was found walled in and standing up-right with his back against the wall. The gilded helmet still bore marks of blows with a sword; Mr. de Helmstädt made a present of this costly armour to the city of Munich. This village in the course of time suffered considerably at many periods,

128

for already under FREDERICK the Victorious, it had felt
the edge of his irresistible sword. In the thirty-years'
war when TILLY had established his head-quarters there,
it suffered equally by friend and foe; and in the war
of the Orleans' succession, it was twice set on fire by
the French, and burnt down as far as the church, the
parsonage, and the Orphan Asylum. At present Handschuchsheim is one of the most flourishing villages of
the Bergsstrasse (chain of mountains from Darmstadt to
Heidelberg and Wiesloch, and the whole length of road
along these mountains). In its environs the fruit ripens
the earliest, and there have been years when the cherries alone have sold for twelve to fifteen hundred florins.
It is also much frequented for its pure air and wholesome situation by persons suffering from diseases of the
chest, who are very often relieved there from their complaint. The collections of Mr. UDE are very interesting,
particularly for the great richness of the Mexican curiosities. This gentleman has a charming country-seat here,
and the grounds have been laid out by the celebrated
horticulturist Thelemann, director of the gardens of the
Duke of Nassau at Biberich. It may perhaps be necessary to mention here that Handschuchsheim and Neuenheim, which we shall notice lower down, as well as many
other villages in the neighbourhood of Heidelberg, are
far more ancient than Heidelberg itself; in the archives
for instance you will find: Handschuchsheim is mentioned in 764, Neuenheim in 765, Kirchheim and Rohrbach in 766 and Eppelheim in 770.

From Handschuchsheim it is a quarter of an hour's
walk along the Bergstrasse [1]) to Neuenheim, a village

[1]) The Bergstrasse or mountain road, is really that road which
leads all the way from Darmstadt to Freiburg; however there was a
second road which led to the left along the Rhine, and was called the
Rhine road or Rheinstrasse. In a more confined view, the road which
leads from Darmstadt to Heidelberg only, is called the Bergstrasse.

enjoying as pure and agreeable an air as Handschuchsheim. To the right, before the wanderer reaches the
village, he will come to a farm consisting of several
buildings called the „Mönchshof" (Monk's farm), which
formerly belonged to the Augustine friars of Heidelberg;
it was here in 1518, three years before the imperial
diet at Worms, that MARTIN LUTHER passed the night
in the miserable hut with the pointed gable-ends. Near
to Neuenheim on the mountain, the remains of a temple,
and other roman antiquities have been dug up.

If the wanderer does not wish to return by the
bridge, he can here cross the Neckar in a ferryboat to
Heidelberg.

IV. WANDERING.

SCHWETZINGEN, MANNHEIM, HEIDELBERG, CONCLUSION.

We have now visited the most interesting places in the immediate vicinity of Heidelberg, and will now conduct the wanderer a little further to SCHWETZINGEN, celebrated for its magnificent garden. I have traversed the beautiful park and gardens of Versailles, and if the waterworks and fountains are on a grander scale and of greater extent, nevertheless the trees here are far more majestic, and the verdure more various which does not contribute a little to the favorable impression, which the whole makes upon the visitor.

From the railway station passing SCHRIEDER's large hotel, we come a little further on to the right to a straight road or alley, laid out by the Elector Charles Louis, and formerly planted with mulberry-trees, intended for the breeding of silkworms. — This alley also deserves attention, for it forms the base of the geographical map of the Palatinate, executed by C. Meier, under the reign of Charles Theodore.

Another road also leads us to Schwetzingen through the villages of Eppelheim and Plankstadt, from the Mannheim Gate (now pulled down), or the west-end of Heidelberg to the Gas-Works where two roads divide, one to the right goes to Mannheim, the other to the left across the Railway and through the above-named villages to the celebrated gardens; where we can alight either at the Hereditary Prince (Erbprinz Hotel), the Eagle

(Adler), Palatinate Hotel (Pfälzer Hof), or the Stag (Hirsch).

At Whitsuntide according to old custom the Feast of Roses is held here, and then the streets of the town are so encumbered with vehicles of every description, for at this time, people from all parts, from 10 to 15 leagues round come hither either in carriages, on horseback or on foot, as if they were going on a pilgrimage, and the little town usually so quiet, is as lively as a large city at its annual fair. The principal branch of industry of the inhabitants of Schwetzingen and its neighbourhood, consists in the cultivation of hops and tobacco, often amounting to a very considerable sum and is a source of great profit to the community. As there are a great quantity of pine-woods in the vicinity, the air impregnated with their evaporation, is considered wholesome for consumptive persons, and many suffering from this evil, by residing here for some time, very often recover their health, which they had thought to have lost for ever.

The garden consists of 210 acres; and takes nearly an hour's time to go the whole round of it. Though formerly there was a park and a hunting lodge here, where the Raugravine of Degenfeld, the beautiful wife of the Elector Charles Louis resided, Charles Theodore was in fact the first who originally laid out these splendid plantations.

The late garden-director Zeyher has the merit of having transformed and newly arranged many parts of the garden.

The entrance to the garden on going through the castle gate, already presents an imposing sight, for we are surrounded with large Orangeries arranged in an extensive semi-circle, the extremities of which terminate in uncommonly tall and deeply shaded alleys.

In the centre immediately before us, we see the

large fountain, surrounded with smaller ones. The largest of these in which Arion is borne on a dolphin, sends up the water to a height of 52 feet. The statue of Arion, as well as the other figures of the fountains were at one time in the gardens of Stanislaus, formerly King of Poland at Luneville, and were bought from there by Charles Theodore after the King's death.

Four vases of Carrara marble are worthy the attention of the lovers of art. Let us now turn from here to the right towards the north, and approach through a most charming bower, the chef-d'œuvre of the whole garden: a lovely Galathea in the Bath, of Carrara marble by CREPELLO, this statue is deservedly considered the finest ornament of the garden.

Not far from this charming figure, in a spot delightfully shaded, on the top of a rock, dripping with water from a running spring, is a figure of Pan playing on his pipes, he seems as if stuck fast on the rock; this is the work of the director of the drawing academy LAMINE. Close by, there is a group of children playing with goats, this must not be overlooked. — To the right over the ditch we perceive the large green-houses, but let us pass beyond, and going along through deeply shaded alleys turn to the right and stop before one of the finest points in the whole garden, the temple of Apollo, which viewed from the east-side, produces a truly enchanting impression. On the top of a high mass of rocks stands the open temple of the god of the muses, supported by Ionic columns. Mystical grottoes surround the height which bears the sanctuary; two nymphs well executed, carry an urn, out of which flows a strong spring clear as crystal, descending from step to step through the middle of the rocks, and disappearing into a spot shaded by trees more than 125 feet high.

It was here — that an old man more than 80 years

old, and he had also been an ocular witness, — told me that the Court of Charles Theodore performed several plays.

In a semi-circle of this sacred wood are six colossal Sphinxes in sandstone by VERSCHAFFELT, each of which, as my venerable cicerone informed me, were portraits of ladies at the Court of Charles Theodore. The statue in the temple of the God of the sun is of Carrara marble, but is not at all admired by connoisseurs in sculpture; the block of marble out of which it was hewn, was first intended for the statue of a saint, when VERSCHAFFELT received orders from Charles Theodore to construct an Apollo out of it. When the statue was finished, and the Prince asked why he touched the strings of the lyre with his left hand, the artist replied, „Your highness, a God must also be able to play upon the lyre with his left hand." — From the temple of Apollo, we proceed to the Bath-house, in which there is a remarkably well executed painting on the ceiling and other paintings worthy of being seen. We must direct the attention of all connoisseurs to this beautiful painting on the ceiling by GUIBAL, painter to the Court of Wurtemberg; it represents Aurora driving Night before her; there is also a Chandelier in porcelain, very artistically composed of garlands and flowers, by a female employed at the former manufactory of porcelain at Frankenthal. On leaving the Bath-house, a shady avenue leads us to the basin of the birds, in the centre of which is the figure of a large horned-owl which throws up water, and several birds artificially made, perched upon trees and sprigs around cast down water from their beaks into the basin below. The artificial view in the perspective is but trifling.

Now, follow me, wanderer, along a canal towards the north, and after passing several bridges, we shall reach the botanical temple. — Pity it is, that a wanton

son of the muses, struck off the nose of one of the
sphinxes keeping watch here! The temple of botany is
a rotunda with a cupola and bears the inscription:

Botanicae Silvestris, An. MDCCLXXVIII.

In the interior there is a female allegorical figure in
Carrara marble with a scroll on which is inscribed:
Caroli Linnæi systema plantarum. Over four altars are
suspended the portraits of Linnæus, Tournefort, Pliny
and Theophrastus. Not far from this little garden temple,
we may observe the beautiful artificial ruin of a roman
aqueduct, where, upon an eminence in the form of a
tower, the wanderer can have a very agreeable view all
over the garden. The lime-tuffs and other rocky stones
on account of their porous nature give to these artificial
ruins a particular ancient appearance.

From here we shall pass the obelisk near the ruin,
it is 45 feet high and proceed towards the large lake,
which likewise owes its picturesque position to the late
Mr. ZEYHER. At the extremity of the grand alley in the
centre, the wanderer will find opposite to him on the
lake two colossal statues of the Rhine and the Danube,
surrounded with children, reeds and waterplants. The
two figures are admirably executed by the able chisel
of VERSCHAFFELT.

The magnificent green lawn or „tapis vert" which is
seen from the lake, surrounded with plantations most
tastefully laid out, offers to the artist rich materials for
the composition of the finest landscapes. But, wanderer,
we will proceed further towards the south, and reach
the modern ruin of the temple of Mercury, which rises
from among the most charming plantations, and produces a very striking and happy effect. From here let
us turn round to the east again, where, after a short,
walk, we arrive at the Grand Mosque, a building which
PIGAGE, the architect, constructed in the genuine style
of Turkish architecture, he having been sent on a jour-

ney to Constantinople in order to accomplish the task confided to him by Charles Theodore, and which he carried out to the perfect satisfaction of the prince.

Before this oriental fane, there is a vestibule supported all round by arabesque pillars, through which you enter the mosque, which is fitted up with great richness and accuracy. Among the sentences or apophthegms which according to the rites of the Moslems are to be seen inscribed all about the temple, some are of a most sublime moral, and Mahometans who visit this building have been seen to bow with veneration before the name of ALLAH, the most high, which is inscribed at the top of the grand portal of the mosque.

The paintings are by J. Quaglio, Stasen and Klotz; the stucco work by the two Pozzi.

From the top of the temple of Mercury which we lately left, the mosque with its two tall minarets is to be seen splendidly reflected in the clear water below. From the two minarets which can be ascended by 127 steps, you have a fine view of the whole garden as well as a distant view over the extensive valley of the Rhine. Near to this mosque is a common well, containing a sulphur spring. We then come to the temple of Minerva where the Goddess of Wisdom in white marble sits enthroned.

The wanderer will meet with many statues in Carrara marble and sandstone, with many other curiosities, which we have no space in this book to designate; but the most of these figures are in very bad taste, nor are they either of any high worth.

But the theatre which is to be seen behind the north wing of the orangeries, is worthy of attention.

A visit to the dressing rooms reminds us of the first dramatic artists of the golden days of the Mannheim stage, for we still here upon the walls see the names of an Iffland, a Beil &c.

But to Schwetzingen is still attached a very sad recollection for a German, for it was here that HEBEL,
the mild and benevolent German poet, the spirited philosopher, the true friend, the social companion whose
conversation was mixed with the most lively expressions
of wit, and one of the noblest and most generous of
men, expired the 22nd September 1826 at the house of
his old friend ZEYHER. The ecclesiastical counsellor and
poet SONNTAG who died lately at Carlsruhe, said formerly of Hebel:

> „Hebel starb — lasst uns dies Wort nicht sagen!
> Sänger, die so schöne Kronen tragen
> Von Parnassus Lorbeern, sterben nie;
> Stürzt, was Staub und Erde ist, zusammen,
> In der Ehrfurcht hohen Opferflammen
> Ehret noch die späte Nachwelt sie.“

> „Hebel died — let us not speak that word!
> Poets who wear such beauteous crowns
> With Parnassus' laurels bound, do never die;
> What dust and earth is, falls together,
> But veneration of their high sacrific flames
> Will ever cause posterity to honor them.“

Two years ago a committee was formed in Mannheim
under the patronage of the privy counsellor NUESSLIN
and the councellor of state BRUNNER, to erect a monument at Schwetzingen to the immortal Hebel, which
has not only met with the most favorable support on
the part of our illustrious Grand-Duke and the Evan-
gelical General Synod, but also from the friends and
admirers of Hebel in and out of Baden, and the sub-
scriptions have already amounted to a very considerable
sum. We cannot forbear making honorable mention
of this committee who have undertaken the generous
task of erecting a monument to one of the noblest men
and distinguished poets of our native country, on the
spot where his ashes repose.

If you should wish to carry with you home some of

the principal views of the garden, I recommend to you the choice collection of Mr. Schwab, the print-seller, who has always a large number on hand; and should you wish to have more detailed information of the numerous objects in this splendid garden, I refer you to Leger's Guide through the Garden of Schwetzingen, edited by C. de Graimberg, Mannheim 1828, as well as Zeyher's and Riger's Descriptions of the Garden and Plantations of Schwetzingen, Mannheim 1809.

Now, respected wanderer, let me conduct you on our road to Mannheim, that beautifully constructed town, and let us behold its present new and flourishing condition. In the period of its first splendour before CHARLES THEODORE left it in 1777 for Munich, Mannheim had a population of 25,000 souls, in 1802 it was reduced to 13,000, and now it has increased again to 25,688, and consequently is the most populous town in the Grand-duchy of Baden, whilst Carlsruhe the place of residence of the Grand-Duke has only 25,163 inhabitants. — Mannheim is increasing daily, which is a sure proof of its flourishing state in commerce, industry and prosperity.

It is situated about 258 feet above the level of the sea upon flooded lands and in 26° 9' 40" longitude and 49° 29' 12" latitude. The lover of botany will find in its neighbourhood many fine plants with which he can enrich his herbal, such as, *Helmenthia echioïdes* (near the Neckar gardens), *Cicuta virosa*, *Comarum palustre* (on the Turf-moor) and the *Sperpula nodosa* (in the damp sand) and in the waters of the Old Rhine the splendid *Nymphaea alba*, *Schweykerta nymphoïdes*, *Tropa natans*, *Ittnera major* and numerous sorts of *Patamajeton*.

We will pass over the legends which exist of the origin of Mannheim, and merely mention that it was already known in the most ancient times, several still very interesting Roman antiquities, which relate to its history having been found there, and it appears that in the archives of the Convent of Lorsch, it already appeared in the eighth century under the name of „MANNINHEIM"; the Elector Frederick IV. raised the old village to a town, fortified it, and erected a strong citadel on the side of the Rhine, called after the name of its founder „Fredericksburg". The plate laid in the foundation stone had a latin inscription, which contained in brief, Mannheim's former history, and runs thus in English:

„Happiness and blessing above all. Frederick IV., Count Palatine of the Rhine, Arch-grand-master of the Holy Roman Empire and Elector, Duke of Bavaria &c. built upon the ground of old Franconian Suabia, at the confluence of the Neckar and the Rhine, where formerly the celebrated Emperor Valentinian had erected a fort against the attacks of the Germans, but which soon fell into the hands of the Franks, and then came into the possession of the Palatinate, for the protection of himself, his people and his country, a very strong castle with bulwarks, and a town entirely new from its foundation, whereupon he with his own hand laid this plate and first stone on the 17th March 1606."

Already in former times, towards the south, and close on the banks of the Rhine, stood the old strong castle of EICHOLZHEIM, where as before related in 1415 Pope John XXIII. was detained prisoner by Louis III. The struggles of the thirty-years' war and that of the succession of Orleans covered Mannheim and the whole of the Palatinate with blood and carnage, and it is Charles Philip alone that can with right be first called the founder of Mannheim's future importance.

The quarrel of this prince with the citizens of Heidelberg and the reformed Consistory in regard to the church of the Holy Ghost, which he exclusively wished to devote to the sole use of catholic worship, intending to give the reformed community a new temple — was the cause of his removing his residence to Mannheim, and he raised that town to a degree of splendour unknown in those times.

On the 2nd July 1790 he laid the foundation stone of the castle which was completed in a short time, and became one of the largest and most beautiful castles of Germany.

The Heidelberg gate which on its demolition in 1806 was sold by auction, was also built by Charles Philip, and had on the outer side a latin inscription, which read thus in English:

„Under the blessing of the most high God, King MANUS gave the name unto this town 370 years after the deluge; the Emperor VALENTINIAN fortified it 372 A. D.; the Elector FREDERICK IV. restored it in 1606; the Elector JOHN WILLIAM in 1698 rose it again from out its ashes; under the reign of the Emperor CHARLES VI., the Elector CHARLES PHILIP of the Palatinate erected this monument of his imperial house and country in the 10th year of the imperial reign 1722."

We only mention this inscription, because it refers like the former one to the earlier history of Mannheim.

After the death of the Elector JOHN WILLIAM, his brother CHARLES PHILIP succeeded him the 8th June 1716 and reigned 26 years; he died on the 31st December 1742 at the age of 81, one of the oldest reigning princes living at that time.

Charles Philip was the last prince of the house of Neuburg, and his successor Charles Theodore of the house of Sulzbach, born 10th December 1724, was but 18 years old, when he took the reins of government. Under this prince Mannheim was raised to its highest glory, for he used every means in his power from the commencement of his reign to advance the prosperity of this town; but towards the end of the XVIII. century it suffered all the horrors of war; the French besieged and bombarded·it in 1794, and the Austrians in 1795. During these sieges many interesting traits took place, which deserve to be transmitted to posterity, and will still do honour to the inhabitants of Mannheim even to this second generation; the short space afforded to us in this work, will only permit our relating one of these circumstances, and which may serve for many others. One may imagine the terror caused by the siege, when it is known that 16,500 large cannon balls, and 6000 of smaller dimensions, 3200 howitzers and 1300 bomb-shells were thrown into the town, and of all the houses only 14 escaped unhurt; when here and there the shells set the houses on fire, and it was no longer allowed to sound the alarm-bell, to call the citizens, to extinguish the flames; it was then that the venerable Dean SPIELBERGER ran from house to house amidst a shower of balls, in order to assemble the people to extinguish the fire. The French commandant caused seven wagons heavily loaded with gunpowder to be brought before the reformed church and left them there; as the houses all around were threatened with destruction, and in case of an explosion, the inhabitants complained of this to general Montaigne, who paid no attention to their complaint, whereupon several courageous citizens dragged these wagons back under a continual fire before the house of the commandant, who immediately ordered them to be taken before the Neckar-gate. The names of these brave men who risked their lives to prevent the total destruction of their town, were MAYER, schoolmaster, ERHARDT, parish clerk, GRIES, stocking weaver, LAMMERT and his brother, bakers, SCHÜTZ, saddler, BERNHARDI, dyer, and two labouring blacksmiths. The misery of the unfortunate inhabitants of Mannheim had now attained its highest point, when at last on the 22nd November the capitulation was concluded upon, and the town surrendered to the Austrians. The bridge of boats at that time destroyed, was only restored in 1814, and furnished with iron boats after the fire of 1849.

CHARLES THEODORE died 16th February 1799, and MAXIMILIAN JOSEPH of the house Palatine of Deux-Ponts ascended the electoral throne. In the same year Mannheim again capitulated to the French, and on the 31st May of that year, the fortifications were begun to be rased and in which the inhabitants of both sexes joyfully took a part. On the 24th August Arch-Duke CHARLES made his entry into the town, afterwards it was alternately taken by the French and then by the Austrians, and had still to suffer many inflictions, the natural consequences of continued war.

On the 23rd November 1802 the Elector MAXIMILIAN JOSEPH relieved the subjects of those countries ceded to Baden of their oath of allegiance to him, and the Elector CHARLES FREDERICK of Baden took possession of them.

All the establishments that CHARLES THEODORE had devoted to arts and sciences have been suspended, with the exception of the Observatory and the Theatre, even the greatest part of the numerous treasures of art, of which Mannheim in its most flourishing state was in possession, were all sent off to Munich, where they still form up to this day the most splendid ornaments in the collections of that city; but however CHARLES FREDERICK did a great deal for Mannheim, by transforming the demolished fortifications into walks and gardens, and by adding to the few remaining paintings in the gallery, all those which are now admired at this present time; he collected a choice assortment of engravings and erected the hall of antiquities.

The two monuments, the one on the Parade-Square and the other on the Market-Place were erected in 1771; the first by order of the Elector JOHN WILLIAM

in Düsseldorf by the celebrated chevalier GABRIEL CRE-
PELLO; it is of metal and weighs 300 cwt.; the subject
in all probability represents time, with all he produces
and consumes; it is greatly overloaded with allegorical
subjects and stands upon a massive pedestal of four
strong projecting pillars joined together in solid arches.
On the pedestal of black and white marble, and constructed according to the direction of BIBIENA, are eight
large stone basins, for the whole was intended originally
to be used as a running fountain. The Elector CHARLES
PHILIP caused the pyramid to be brought from Düsseldorf and made it a present to the town. In 1840 and
1841 the monument was quite restored and closed in
with an iron railing.

The second mentioned monument on the market-
place is from the chisel of P. VON DER BRANDEN and
his son MATTHEW, finished in 1767 and was erected in
Schwetzingen. The Elector CHARLES THEODORE made
a present of this monument to the town of Mannheim
in 1771. It represents the four elements, and was intended like the former to ornament a fountain, which it
does at present. A third monument erected to the memory of the veterans of the Baden army, stands upon
the square opposite to the arsenal.

The new free port or haven begun in 1834 and
finished in 1840 in honour of the accession of the Grand-
duchy of Baden to the German Zollverein or commercial tariff-union, has contributed materially to the increasing prosperity of Mannheim as a commercial town.
In 1840 the railway to Heidelberg, and in 1846 the
Maine-Neckar-Railway were first opened, and on the
15th November 1844, the fête of his late Royal Highness
the Grand-Duke LEOPOLD of Baden, the new chain-
bridge over the Neckar was inaugurated, and opened to
the public, and already in 1841 the first steam-boat appeared on the Neckar.

Having now mentioned the principal historical events of Mannheim, I will proceed to inform the visitor to the town, of all it contains that may be interesting, and begin with the Castle, a beautiful edifice, built as we have already mentioned by CHARLES PHILIP, but suffered very much during the bombardment; it is now in the greatest part restored. It extends from where the Rhine flows by Mannheim nearly the whole width of the town. In 1795 so fatal for Mannheim, a whole wing of this splendid castle was burnt entirely to the ground, and with it a valuable collection of physical and meteorological instruments, and the Italian opera house with all its beautiful scenery and decorations painted by Quaglio. At present one part of the castle, namely the left wing is occupied by her Imperial Highness the Dowager Grand - Duchess STEPHANIE of Baden (widow of the Grand-Duke Charles), while the right wing is set apart for the residence of his Royal Highness the Grand-Duke Frederick and many other personages attached to the government; moreover many valuable collections such as:

The Picture - Gallery, containing more than 300 oil paintings, amongst which are several celebrated works, f. ex. a descent from the cross by Lesueur, two beautiful paintings by Everding and many other original paintings by great masters. There is a beautiful collection of 19,000 engravings, and the rooms appropriated to the antiquities contain a great number of very interesting objects for the historian and antiquary. — The magnificent treasures of art and nature which were preserved here formerly, when Mannheim was called the Athens of Germany, have all been removed to Munich as we have mentioned before; but in our time a great deal has been done to enrich the Cabinet of Natural History; the collection of Petrefactions is very large, COLLIN collected them in his time from all parts of Europe, and which for the most part are still here and lately arranged in order. The collection of shells and corals deserve particular attention. This cabinet of natural history is under the direction of the Aulic counsellor and professor Kilian under whose able management the cabinet is sure to be continually improved and enlarged.

The castle also contains many magnificent apartments, with fine painted ceilings by Quaglio and all the floors most beautifully inlaid; the chapel of the castle at the end of the left wing is a fine structure; the painting on the ceiling is by Asam and that at the high altar by Gotreau. The great treasures of this chapel, such as, the pix of pure Rhine gold, and the magnificent altar dedicated to St. Hubert of massive silver, have been transmitted with other church treasures to Munich.

The Castle-Gardens are also laid out very tastefully and close adjoining to them is the favorite bath and house of entertainment called the Rhein-Lust.

Amongst the churches of Mannheim the church of the Jesuits built under CHARLES THEODORE from 1733 to 1756 deserves particular attention for the magnificent manner in which it is fitted up. The church is 250 feet in length, 107 feet in breadth, and 108 feet in height. The sculpture work is by Verschaffelt mentioned before at Schwetzingen, the altar-piece by Grahe, the plan by Bibiena and the bells by Speck of Heidelberg. The Elisabeth Bell is perhaps one of the finest toned bells in Europe. — The latin inscription on the foundation stone when translated into english reads thus:

„To the one and triune God. In veneration of the service of the blessed virgin Mary, conceived without sin. In veneration of the service of all the Saints; to show a veneration for divine service, in order to animate and to instil into my subjects the catholic devotion, and the true knowledge of faith, when Clement XII. held the keys of heaven upon earth, Charles VI. ruled over the roman empire, the foundation stone of this court church was laid, and built in honor of St. Ignatius of Loyola, and St. Francis Xavier, destined for the service of the society of Jesus in the year 1733 — 111 years after their canonization on the same day of the year by Charles Philip, Count Palatine of the Rhine and Elector, the most obedient son of the catholic church, and the humblest servant of God and the Saints."

This splendid church is a noble monument of Mannheim, and its interior is not only rich, but abundantly decorated with paintings, gildings and sculpture in black and white marble, the latter the work of VERSCHAFFELT are particularly distinguished, and the tabernacle of the high altar is shown as a mineralogical curiosity.

The other churches of Mannheim are not celebrated as buildings of high art.

The Jesuit-college, now the lyceum, was built in 1739. —

There was formerly in Mannheim an Italian Opera and a French Theatre; in the latter several pieces of Voltaire were represented for the first time before they appeared in Paris. The present theatre which occupies a whole square of the town, was built under CHARLES THEODORE from a plan by Quaglio, who painted the beautiful scenery; it dates its foundation in 1778. To this theatre are attached many great and pleasing recollections, when the german dramatic art was in its bloom, for here SCHILLER [1]) was engaged as dramatic poet, the intellectual VON DALBERG presided as director of the institution till 1803, and the names of IFFLAND, BEIL, BECK, RENSCHUB and BÖCKH will for ever shine in the history of the german stage as stars of the first magnitude.

Lately this building has been considerably enlarged

---

[1]) Schiller lived in the house called „Karlsberg" in the parade square, now occupied by Mr. Frisch, print-seller.

146

and newly decorated under the able and skilful direction of Mühldörfer, and may be considered as one of the handsomest theatres in Europe.

The Kaufhaus or Merchant's-hall, was built in 1736 from a plan by Alexander Bibiena. This edifice is built on piles and forms the whole of the square Nr. 1.

The Arsenal is also worthy the attention of the lovers of architecture, being built in a noble style from a plan of VERSCHAFFELT's under CHARLES THEODORE in 1777.

The Observatory, situated to the north behind the Jesuit's-college, was completed in 1779; it is 111 feet high, and provided with excellent astronomical instruments. There are also several private collections of paintings, curiosities, coins and antiquities to which strangers can easily gain admittance on applying to the respective proprietors. The Jews' Synagogue built in pure style by the late land surveyor and builder Lendorf and finished in 1855 is worthy of admiration. The tram railroad lately constructed passes all round the town, and communicating the ports of the Rhine and the Neckar with the stations of the Baden and Maine-Neckar railways has greatly contributed in forwarding the commerce of Mannheim. There is only one thing to be desired, and which would be of incalculable advantage to the prosperity of Mannheim, that the projected plan of a stone bridge across the Rhine be soon carried into execution.

By the description of Mannheim I have just given, my intention was only to inform the stranger of what was worthy of being seen there, and for further information I refer him to a more complete description by Rieger: „Beschreibung von Mannheim", Mannheim 1824; and likewise a little work very ingeniously written and chronologically arranged, entitled: „Mannheims Denkwürdigkeiten seit dessen Entstehung bis zur neuesten

Zeit von J. P. Walther, Mannheim im Bürgerhospitale 1855"; and conclude this wandering with the words of a poet who speaks thus of Mannheim:

"Sei mir gegrüsst, Du schöne Frau im Glanze,
Den Dir Gewerbfleiss nun und Handel schenkt,
Dein Gürtel fiel, wie die bewehrte Schanze,
Der uns'rer Väter noch mit Grau'n gedenkt;
Wo düst're Keller nur ihr Leben schirmte,
Und Tod und Jammer riesengross sich thürmte.

Zwei kräft'ge Brüder halten Dich umschlungen
Und bieten Dir der Länder Schätze dar,
Und jener Kunstsinn, der Dich stets durchdrungen,
Er blühet noch, als wie vor sechzig Jahr;
Er ist Dir heimisch, fliehet nie von dannen,
Und glänzt als Kron' der edlen Stadt der M a n n e n.

Sei mir gegrüsst, Du heiliges Asyle,
Das Du der Kunst und Wissenschaft geschenkt!
Sei mir gegrüsst an meiner Wand'rung Ziele,
Mein Geist sich ganz an jene Stätte denkt,
Wo S c h i l l e r einst und Iffland's Muse wohnte,
Der Künste Glanz, des Wissens Krone thronte. [1])

(Richard Wanderer).

If till now, in all my wanderings, which I have made either from the Heidelberg castle, or from Hei-

---

[1]) Hail! beauteous fair one! transplendent with the fame with which industry and commerce crowns thee; thy girdle fell like thy strong fortress which our fathers still remember with terror; when thy dark vaults sheltered them from danger, and death and misery rose up like giants round about.

Two powerful brothers now embrace thee, and offer thee the treasures of the land, and that taste for arts which ever did inspire thee, flourishes with thee still, as it did sixty years ago; it is born within thee, it never will desert thee, and will ever form the brilliant crown of the noble town of M a n!

Hail! sacred asylum, devoted to arts and science, I greet thee! having now reached the end of my pilgrimage, my spirit transports itself to that spot where Schiller lived and Iffland's muse resided, to where art doth flourish and the crown of science is enthroned.

delberg itself, I have omitted giving any particular
description of the latter, it is because in all my relations of the castle as well as its environs, the town of
Heidelberg has been so often mentioned, that I did not
like to make too many repetitions, so I have therefore
chosen the end of my little work to relate what more
I have to say about the town.

Heidelberg, the charming city of the muses is
situated 49^0 $24'$ latitude and 26^0 $18'$ longitude, 300 feet
above the level of the sea on the left bank of the Neckar
from east to west; 2756 yards in length from the Mannheim to the Charles' gate; has at present a population
of 15,061 souls including the resident strangers, and its
population increases every year.

The University of Heidelberg is one of the most
ancient in Germany and was founded as we have already mentioned by RUPERT I. in 1346; for according
to accounts given to us by documents of authority, we
can assume that the Count Palatine RUPERT I. had
already during the life of his brother the Elector RU-
DOLPH II., organised an institution for the cultivation
of science, and had thereby laid the foundation for the
university; but that institution had long remained of
little importance, either for want of means, or not kno-
wing how to employ those it possessed, so that it really
enjoyed no veritable existance; but when RUPERT I.
eventually became (1353) the sole Regent of the Palatinate of the Rhine, he protected his former creation in
every respect, and at last in 1386 raised it to the rank
of a university, he having the year before received the
bull of authorization from Pope URBAN VI. with the
knowledge and consent of his nephew RUPERT II., and
that of the son of the latter RUPERT III. already arrived
at manhood, and on which occasion the celebrated
MARSILIM of INGHEN was appointed first rector of this
new university.

The thirty-years' war, the war of the succession of Orleans and finally the revolution of France in 1789 had injured this celebrated institution during those different periods so considerably, that it was not till Heidelberg eventually came under the sceptre of Baden, that the university obtained a thorough reform under the government of the Grand-Duke CHARLES FREDERICK of glorious memory, and at the present day it is not only reckoned one of the most ancient, but still more, one of the most renowned universities of Germany.

We have drawn the above mentioned authentic historical notes of the University of Heidelberg from a work of the Director of the Lyceum and Aulic Counsellor HAUTZ, a work as yet unpublished, and we can only express our desire that the author may be enabled shortly to commit it to the press, so that we may thereby have a work which will contribute much to the history of science and the learned men of the whole of the Rhine Palatinate; our venerable university would then be no longer deprived of a special history, which the universities of Vienna, Prague, Rostock, Tübingen, Göttingen and others have long since enjoyed.

The University-Library contains a collection of 200,000 volumes of printed works, about 2000 manuscripts, 1000 archives and 60,000 dissertations; besides a collection of old coins, and a number of models in plaster of Paris from the most celebrated antiques.

The Cabinet of Natural History, the Cabinet of Physic, the Theatre of Anatomy, the Clinical Hospital, the Botanical Garden and other learned establishments.

The University of Heidelberg is generally frequented upon an average by about 600 students, and its halls have continually been sending out distinguished men to propagate the light of science into the world even from its commencement as well as up to the present day.

The society called the Museum, is furnished with

periodicals of every description, and is as well as the Harmony easy of access to the stranger; the newspapers and libraries of both these establishments contribute a great deal to the entertainment of the visitors.

The Theatre erected in 1853, and decorated in a very tasteful style affords a fund of amusement and re-creation to the inhabitants of Heidelberg and to strangers. We must however not forget to mention here the choice Collection of Antiques belonging to BAMBERGER, in the Corn Market, where a great many interesting articles are always to be found, and continually draw the attention of the strangers and inhabitants.

The town also has spared no pains in constructing excellent roads and walks in the neighbourhood of Hei-delberg so as to render every interesting spot accessible, thereby considerably improving every point of view, and it has not hesitated to make great sacrifices, which de-serve a grateful acknowledgment.

The Hotels of Heidelberg may be ranked amongst the best in the country, and the Hotels-garnis or Fa-mily-hotels, partly situated on the Anlage or New Pro-menade, and in other parts of the town, afford every necessary comfortable arrangement.

Our great poet JEAN PAUL calls the town of Heidel-berg, the GREAT HOTEL OF GERMANY, and really the philosophic poet is in the right; for in Heidelberg there is annually such an influx of strangers from all countries of the earth, and which constantly increases every year, so that in some measure according to the words of the poet, the town may be said to be transformed into one large hotel.

I believe I may safely predict, that Heidelberg is looking forward to a greater futurity; its charming si-tuation, with a little aid, and some necessary arrange-ments of which it is yet deprived, it may one day become a european place of meeting of strangers from all parts of the world.

I conclude my work with the words of the poet RICHARD WANDERER, who makes the town of Heidelberg say to its castle:

„Du Zierde meiner Höhen, Du Schloss voll Herrlichkeit,
Du stehest noch als Zeuge vergang'ner alter Zeit;
Und siehst auf mich hernieder, wie neu mein Bau erglüht,
Wie RUPRECHT's hohe Schule noch immer herrlich blüht.
Wenn Deine Thürme sinken, zerfallen sind im Graus,
So streut mein Bau noch immer des Wissens Früchte aus." [1]

---

[1] Ornament of my heights, thou magnificent castle, thou remain'st still a witness of the past, thou lookest down upon me from above, and seest my building shine with new lustre, how RUPERT's University still flourishes gloriously; when thy towers have fallen and crumbled into dust, my edifice will still spread out the fruits of knowledge.

152

CHRONOLOGICAL TABLE

OF ALL THE REIGNING PRINCES OF THE PALATINATE OF THE RHINE.

	Born	Died
1. **Conrad of Hohenstaufen** was invested with the Electoral dignity by his brother the Emperor FREDERICK I. (BARBAROSSA) after the death of the Count Palatine HERMANN of STAHLECK. Conrad married IRMENGARD, COUNTESS of HENNEBERG and had issue a daughter AGNES .	1127	1195
2. **Henry**, the Guelph, son of HENRY the LION (Duke of Brunswick) married AGNES Conrad's daughter, and became Palsgrave of the Rhine, CONRAD of HOHENSTAUFEN having after the death of his sons transformed his possessions into female fiefs; this prince abdicated in favour of his son in 1211	1169	1227
3. **Henry**, the Younger, married MATHILDA of BRABANT, and died without issue. .	1194	1214
4. **Louis I.**, Duke of Bavaria, was invested with the Electoral dignity by the Emperor for signal services; but only considered himself as administrator of the Palatinate, for Henry the Younger's father, HENRY the GUELPH heir to CONRAD of HOHENSTAUFEN was still living, until the youngest daughter of Henry the Guelph married his son. His eldest daughter married the Margravine HERMANN of BADEN. The wife of Louis I.		

	Born	Died
was Ludomilla, daughter of Wladislaus, King of Hungary	1174	1231
5. **Otho**, the Illustrious, son of Louis I. married AGNES the youngest daughter of HENRY the GUELPH, and became Count Palatine of the Rhine	1206	1253
6. **Louis II.**, the Severe, son of OTHO first married MARY of BRABANT, whom he had beheaded innocently in a fit of jealousy; then ANNA of SILESIA, and after her death, for the third time he married MATHILDA, daughter of the Emperor RUDOLPH of HABSBURG	1229	1294
7. **Rudolph I.**, son of Louis at the beginning reigned in common with his brother LOUIS the BAVARIAN, who afterwards became Emperor; he divided his lands and retained the Palatinate of the Rhine, while his brother kept Bavaria. He married MATHILDA, daughter of the Emperor ADOLPH of NASSAU; lived in enmity with his imperial brother, came under the ban of the Empire and died in exile. He was the founder of the Rudolph's-building on the Jetta-Bühl .	1274	1319
8. **Adolphus**, the Just, married IRMENGARD of OETTINGEN and was newly invested with the Electoral dignity by his uncle the Emperor LOUIS in 1320	1300	1327
9. **Rudolph II.**, brother of ADOLPH married ANNA of CARINTHIA	1306	1353
10. **Rupert I.**, the Elder, also surnamed RUFUS, reigned according to the will of his uncle, the Emperor Louis in common with his brother for himself and for the son of their deceased brother Adolphus. He was the founder of the University of Heidelberg 1346 and built the Rupertina-chapel of Heidelberg castle, married first with ELISABETH of NAMUR and then with BEATRICE of BERG	1309	1390

154

	Born	Died
11. **Rupert II.**, the Hard-Hearted, son of Adolph, an impetuous warrior, married Beatrice of Sicily	1325	1398
12. **Rupert III.**, surnamed the Good, and on account of his love of justice, called Justinian; the only son of Rupert II., beloved by the princes of his time and the people; he was elected King of Germany in 1400, by the electoral princes at Boppart, after King Wenzel, the Idler was deposed; prudent and brave he knew how to establish order in the interior of the empire. He married Elisabeth, daughter of Frederick IV., Burgrave of Nuremberg. He constructed the Rupert's-building in the castle of Heidelberg. Under his reign the second division of the hereditary lands of Wittelsbach took place, whereby his sons, 1) Louis, had the Palatinate, 2) John, Neuburg, 3) Stephen, Simmern and Deux-Ponts and 4) Otho, Mosbach .	1352	1410
13. **Louis III.**, surnamed the Bearded, the ancestor of the Heidelberg line. He was the patron of the grand Council of Constance in 1414, and confined Pope John XXIII., Balthazar Cossa for a long time in the Rudolph's-building as prisoner. He was married first with Blanch of England and afterwards with Mathilda of Savoy and Piedmont. .	1376	1437
14. **Louis IV.**, surnamed the Candid, married Margaret of Savoy	1424	1449
15. **Frederick I.**, the Victorious, brother of the former, was immediately after the death of his brother Administrator of the Palatinate, but became Elector by the pressing solicitations of his vassals, and won for himself, by his victorious battles against most of the german princes, the Emperor and the Pope, an		

	Born	Died
heroic name in history. He married with the left hand CLARA of DETTIN. He was the builder of the so-called exploded tower, the library and the lower part of the octagon tower	1425	1476
16. **Philip**, the Sincere, son of LOUIS IV. married MARGARET of LANDSHUT, and was a prince devoted to the sciences .	1448	1508
17. **Louis V.**, surnamed the Pacific, for he tried unceasingly at all the several meetings and diets of the Empire, to pacify all those princes who differed in their religious opinions, he was the son of PHILIP and married SYBILLA of BAVARIA. In spite of his love of peace, he nevertheless thought of the hour of peril, and caused all the most important fortifications of the castle of Heidelberg to be constructed, viz.: the grand rampart, the Louis-tower, the watch-tower and the big tower, all these remarkable buildings were united in their time by strong protected subterranean passages; he also constructed the Louis-building. Under his reign the lightning struck the old castle on the little Gaisberg, the gunpowder magazine that was kept there took fire, and the whole building was blown up	1478	1544
18. **Frederick II.**, the Wise, brother of Louis V., completed the fortifications, built the New Court and married DOROTHEA of DENMARK and SWEDEN	1482	1550
19. **Otho Henry**, the Magnanimous, was so called because he generously protected the arts and sciences; he was the builder of the most beautiful architectural monument of the castle of Heidelberg, the Otho-Henry-Building; he married SUSANNA of BAVARIA	1502	1559
20. **Frederick III.**, the Pious, of the house		

156

	Born	Died
of Simmern, married MARY of BRANDEN-BURG	1515	1576
21. **Louis VI.**, son of the former, married ELISABETH of HESSEN, afterwards ANNA of EAST-FRIESLAND	1539	1583
22. **John Casimir**, a chivalrous prince, became administrator of the Palatinate after his brother Louis' death, married ELISABETH of SAXONY; he was the builder of the first Big Tun and its cellar . . .	1543	1592
23. **Frederick IV.**, son of LOUIS VI., married LOUISA JULIANA of NASSAU-ORANGE, and erected the splendid Frederick's building with the new chapel.	1574	1610
24. **Frederick V.**, surnamed the Patient, married ELISABETH STUART of ENGLAND, grand-daughter of the unfortunate Queen MARY STUART. He built on the strong covered batteries of Louis V. the palace of Elisabeth or the English building, the noble style of which is still to be seen in the ruins, and ornamented the environs of the castle with splendid gardens. He was elected King of Bohemia and was invested the 23rd October 1619 with the regal diadem at Prague; but already in 1620 he lost a battle at the White Mountain near Prague against the Emperor Ferdinand, together with his crown, fled with his wife to Holland, and died without ever more returning to the castle of his ancestors	1596	1632
25. **Charles Louis**, surnamed the German Solomon, returned to his hereditary lands in 1649, restored the castle almost ruined by the ravages and flames of the thirty-years' war, endeavoured with all the means in his power to re-estabish the prosperity of his country which had been so cruelly afflicted, and soon succeeded, for the richness of its soil materially		

	Born	Died
assisted him. He was a noble prince; married CHARLOTTE of HESSEN-CASSEL, from whom he was separated, and then married with the left hand, the beautiful LOUISA, Baroness DEGENFELD. He died on his way from Mannheim to Heidelberg in an orchard in the village of Edingen	1617	1680
26. **Charles**, the only son and heir of the former, married WILHELMINA ERNESTINA of DENMARK. This prince dying without leaving any issue, and his sister being married to the Duke of ORLEANS, brother of King LOUIS XIV., the death of the Elector was the signal for that unfortunate war, which brought nothing but devastation and terror over the whole of the Palatinate	1651	1688
27. **Philip William**, of the house of Neuburg, married first with CATHARINE of POLAND, then with ELISABETH AMELIA of HESSEN-DARMSTADT. This prince was already 70 years of age when he came to the electoral throne; he died at Vienna at his eldest daughter's, wife of the Emperor Leopold	1615	1690
28. **John William**, eldest son of the former; under his reign the beautiful Palatinate became a desert through the wars of the succession of Orleans; consequently JOHN WILLIAM lived in Düsseldorf, where he energetically acted towards the revival of the Palatinate. Married first with MARIA ANNA of AUSTRIA, afterwards with ANNA JOSEPHA of FLORENCE	1658	1716
29. **Charles Philip**, brother of the former, married CHARLOTTE of RADZIVIL, and secondly THERESIA CATHARINA, daughter of the Polish Prince Joseph Lubomirsky. Contentions having arisen between the Reformed Consistory and the citizens of		

	Born	Died
Heidelberg with respect to the church of the Holy Ghost, caused this prince to remove his court to Mannheim, and built the beautiful castle there. He restored the castle of Heidelberg as much as possible	1661	1742

30. **Charles Theodore**, of the house of Sulzbach, a collateral branch of the line of Neuburg, the nearest relative to his predecessor, a prince devoted to the fine arts; under his reign Mannheim prospered considerably. He built the Charles' Gate in Heidelberg, as well as the beautiful bridge over the Neckar, and had the intention of entirely restoring the castle of Heidelberg and fixing his residence there, when the lightning struck the New Building on the 24th June 1764 and burnt the castle down to the walls; afterwards he caused roofs to be erected over several of the buildings to preserve them from total ruin. To him the present Big Tun owes its existence. In 1777 he inherited the throne of Bavaria, and removed his court to Munich; with him the line of the Palatinate-Sulzbach became extinct, this prince having died without heirs. He was married first to ELISABETH AUGUSTA of SULZBACH, and afterwards to MARIA LEOPOLDINA of AUSTRIA . . . . — 1724 — 1799

31. **Maximilian Joseph**, of the younger branch of the line of the Schyres, and the house of Deux-Ponts. In virtue of the treaty of peace of Luneville in 1801, this prince was, according to a particular decree of the princes of the empire in 1802 to 1803 obliged to transfer the land, with the venerable castle of his ancestors, to the newly established electoral house of BADEN. In 1806 he be-

	Born	Died
came King of BAVARIA and married first MARY WILHELMINA AUGUSTA of HESSEN-DARMSTADT, and secondly FREDERICA WILHELMINA CAROLINE of BADEN . .	1756	1824
32. **Charles Frederick**, first Elector of Baden and Count Palatine of the Rhine, one of the greatest princes of his time, became Grand-Duke in 1806; married 1) CAROLINE LOUISA, born Landgravine of HESSEN-DARMSTADT, 2) LOUISA CAROLINE, Countess of HOCHBERG . . .	1728	1811
33. **Charles Louis Frederick**, grand-son of the former, Grand-Duke, married STEPHANIE LOUISA ADRIENNE, adopted daughter of the Emperor Napoleon I. This prince was the founder of the Baden Constitution	1786	1818
34. **Louis William Augustus**, son of CHARLES FREDERICK, Grand-Duke	1763	1830
35. **Leopold**, Grand-Duke, son of CHARLES FREDERICK. This illustrious prince, one of the most excellent regents of the land, did a great deal towards the preservation of the splendid ruins of the castle of Heidelberg. He married SOPHIA of SWEDEN . . , ...	1790	1852
37. **Frederick William Louis**, Grand-Duke, married Her Royal Highness the Princess LOUISA of PRUSSIA, 20th September 1856.	1826	—

THE GRAND TOUR

THROUGH THE RUINS OF THE HEIDELBERG CASTLE.

———

Before I point out this tour to the wanderer, I must beg leave to remark it can only be made with a large party, for it takes the accompanying guide nearly half a day to go his round; nevertheless it is in every respect of great interest, and will produce upon him a lasting impression, by the romantic and picturesque points which it offers.

The little tour comprises all the principal buildings, with the exception of the ascent of the octagon-tower.

	Letters and numbers.	Page.
We will now enter		
1) **Rupert's Building** then pass to . .	C.	19
2) **Rudolph's Building** or the old building over the castle wall to the	A.	12
3) **Covered-Battery** to the falconet battery and from here through the little	w.	75
4) **Wicket-Gate** towards the Artillery-park into the	x.	76
5) **Guard-room** near the big tower then to the	z.	76
6) **Dining-room**, afterwards called the pleasure-garden, from here we shall ascend the wooden staircase up to the	P.	63
7) **Big tower** and then back to the . .	H.	36
8) **Dining-room** through the Elisabeth-building over the w o o d e n b r i d g e of the cooperage to the	P.	64
9) **Church**, from then to the	O.	57
10) **Cellar of the Great Tun**, then through the	N. 1.	49
11) **Postern**-gate to the outlet on the left up the steps into the	t.	75

162

From this tower which commands the greatest part of the round we have just made, we have in every direction a bird's eye view of all we have seen and described. Towards the east the Friesenberg, the gigantic creation of Solomon de Caus, the Königsstuhl and the Valley of the Neckar; more towards the south the Molkenkur and the Gaisberg, while to the west we can perceive a part of the town, the vast plain of the Rhine and the mountains beyond; at last to the north of the town we perceive the Neckar, Neuenheim and the Heiligenberg; we will therefore close our Guide here at the Quadrangular watch-tower in order to make a total impression of the whole upon our respected wanderer, so that he may be enabled to recollect all he has seen. On taking leave of my readers, I will still mention, that in case any new diggings or important discoveries should be made, I shall not fail to annex them by way of addition to my little work, which in conclusion, I beg respectfully to recommend.

INDEX.

164

Breinigsville, PA USA
02 February 2011
254672BV00003B/17/P